132+ Delicious Salads, Dressings And Dips

More Than 132 Delicious, Adaptable Salads, Dressings And Dips – Gabrielle's FUSS-FREE Healthy Veg Recipes With Easy-To-Find Ingredients

By Gabrielle Raiz

Thanks for purchasing this book, I hope you love it! If you do like the book, then please review the book on Amazon – it will help me improve and make each version even better as well as keep writing more books for you!

Gabrielle Raiz is the author of the best-selling book & DVD *"Hot Yoga MasterClass"* and the Principal of the Hot Yoga Teacher Training Program *"Hot Yoga Doctor Pro"*.

Visit my other sites!

http://www.HotYogaDoctor.com/

http://www.HotYogaMasterClass.com/

http://www.EasyHotYogaWeightloss.com/

http://www.HotYogaTeacher.com/

Keep your recipes and your book up to date!

To get more tips and techniques for making **Delicious Salads, Dressings And Dips**, join my **Healthy Salads Newsletter** (it's free!) – just use the link below. I'll also let you know when new versions are released – which will be free for you of course!

http://www.hotyogadoctor.com/salads-newsletter

Other books by Gabrielle on Amazon!

Salads

Introduction: No More Boring Salads!

Salads are under-rated by many. Many people treat them as the 'thing on the side that you <u>should</u> eat' and they eat a hot meal as their main nutrition. I know because that used to be me! But salads can be the most amazing main part of your meal and I want to show you how!

This book was written especially for the uninspired and salad-bored majority who are tired of the same old lettuce, tomato, onion concoction with a few embellishments. Maybe you have a store-bought dressing or 2 in your fridge that you use for every vegetable combination. No wonder the salad pizzazz has gone. Or maybe it was never there.

Well! Worry no more. There is a way out from the tedium. You can make incredible salads with less than a handful of ingredients in total, that will knock your proverbial socks off! And you can make sophisticated salads that will delight your taste buds too.

Your satisfaction is only limited by your willingness to experiment and appreciate the many ideas and guidelines in this book.

But making salads is just half the story! What you dress your salad with can revitalize your palate and revolutionize your meals. When you use interesting, scrumptious dressings, they can transform just about ANY vegetable into the taste sensation you have been craving.

In this book you'll find a range of salads. From the simple to the sophisticated in terms of numbers of ingredients and complexity and types of inclusions. What will really get your appetite going is when you discover the world of dressings (including salsas and dips) and how to pair them with your salads.

This is why you'll find more dressings and dips in this book than the actual salad recipes.

I hope you are inspired to know that you can eat a salad with just about any vegetable in it. You can choose your ingredients based on creating deliciously nutritious blends.

But rest assured, that even if you find yourself with little more than the humble lettuce, onion and tomato in your fridge one day, that you'll find a cornucopia of amazing things to dress them with – and be excited about it.

What about my salad-phobic children?

What children are served when they are very young really can pave the way to the tastes that they develop (naturally). Because of the cultural leanings and fast food availability (which have become cultural habits) many children are salad-resistant and don't eat nearly enough raw vegetables and fruit and green leafy vegetables.

Your journey with your children in mind, will involve finding innovative ways to tempt them. You may find simple vegetable sticks with crazy, delicious and interesting dips and thicker dressings could be the key.

The other wonderful way is to front load them with green smoothies. These are pretty much salads in a glass that are extremely kid-friendly (aka people-friendly) that provide the nutrition along with the sweetness of fruit.

I have found with my own family that using green smoothies has made our daughter way more interested in experimenting with salads. My goal of providing her with the best nutrition I can is made so much easier.

If you need a quick, easy and delicious stepping stone to incredible nutrition, then please also take a look at my other book called "Green Smoothie Magic". It's a bestseller that has been delighting thousands around the world.

This series of cooking and food preparation books is something that I am in the throes of creating, that combines my love of great food, simplicity and ease. It's important to me that the recipes are highly adaptable to you and your needs and that you can find just about any of the ingredients within these pages at your supermarket and your local farmers' market.

So, let's take a look at sensational salads...

Contents

Making Super Salads

Something I learned about two decades ago when I read Lesley and Susannah Kenton's book "Raw Energy" is that if you want to really enjoy the flavors of your vegetables then cut them very small. Seems silly that a small detail (pardon the pun) would make such an impression on me.

Out of that was born one of our family favorites – "The Super Salad".

You don't always have to cut everything small. The trick is to prepare your vegetables *differently*. It's not very attractive (for the eyes, the palate or the stomach) for every salad you eat to look the same.

Friends of mine, Laurentine and James who produced the world famous Food Matters movie and the Hungry For Change movie, told me in an interview for my yoga website (http://www.HotYogaDoctor.com) that a simple, fantastic way of really amping up the quality of your food intake is to "Add A Salad".

Add a salad

This simple rule is one that can transform your eating habits and your health. It came as a big relief to distill the path to vibrant health to something so incredibly easy. Of course, creating some reasonable variety is still key.

If you've been making the same old salad with the same bottled vinaigrette then it is exciting to know that you can make changes easily. This is what this book is about.

So, adding a salad can help you make a different taste. But just imagine for a moment that each of the 3 salads on your table is prepared with your garden variety grater. I can tell you that not only will it not look very appealing it will feel 'same old same old' (boring) in the mouth.

If every mouthful *feels* the same then your experience is going to lose its appeal very quickly ... even if the salads are different.

Having different ways to prepare your veggies is a gift. Thankfully there are lots of very inexpensive gadgets that will help you be creative. Read on for some excellent ideas on how to create the perception of different salads just by varying the texture.

How to vary your salads and tempt your senses

Below you'll find some lists of the different ingredients you can put in your salads. Run your eye over them, get inspired. At the very least, the lists may remind you of items that may have slipped out of your awareness. You will enjoy getting reacquainted with them or make some new 'friends'. Then it's up to you to decide if you will follow a salad recipe, make substitutions or make up your own. You're here for some salad and dressing recipes. So I will assume you want to start with mine!

A major 'secret' to pepping up your experiences is in what you do. Prepare your ingredients in different ways to create interest and excitement so your food continues to surprise and delight you.

Think about ...

- Slicing
- Cubing
- Spiral grating
- Grating
- Julienne cutting or julienne grating with an implement (into matchsticks)
- Using your peeler to slice finely, as in long fine ribbons
- Supreme cutting citrus (a technique to remove the pith, detailed in this book)
- Juicing
- Mashing
- Or even lightly grilling or steaming

... your ingredients

A very useful tool is a mandolin slicer. They have all sorts of blades so that you can slice thick and thin and in between, you can julienne (matchsticks), you can grate.

Look into Spiral graters, Julienne graters (for small jobs) and also invest in a good knife. I also have a little handheld implement that I use to 'crinkle cut' cucumber, zucchini and carrot. It's got a wavy edge. You can use a peeler to peel and a peeler to make strips of veggies too.

If you'd like to see my recommended resources (with links to most of the recommendations) – Blenders, Graters, Knives and various helpful kitchen gear to save you time and improve your results, then please check out this special page I have put together for you:

http://www.hotyogadoctor.com/kitchen-resources

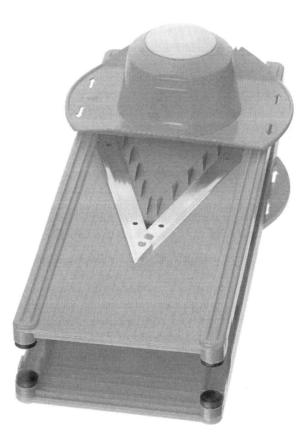

We've just purchased a handy little electric grater and slicer that is way easier to use and clean up than a food processor. It's a Tefal Fresh Express. I am not sure if this is available everywhere in the world so do some shopping around.

Get creative. Have fun with your food. Connect with its energy, its vibrancy, its frequency and its nutrition.

Practising yoga (and if you don't know, I am known the world over as a yoga expert and my moniker is 'Hot Yoga Doctor') is about being consciously aware of your actions. It's called being in the moment. It's definitely a big part of living a fulfilling life. I like to take those principles to every part of my existence including making food, eating it … and cleaning up afterward!

So enjoy the sensual process of preparing your food *and* eating it.

Having a healthy enjoyment of (healthy) food will manifest a healthy relationship with all food. It will also create a healthy body shape. That's an important consideration for the many millions who need help with that. Many people start a yoga practice or begin exercising because they want to change their shape by toning up and/or slimming down.

I believe strongly that eating consistently well creates increasingly better choices and reduces cravings for things that do not serve you. This is quite literally a sign that you are becoming increasingly in tune with what you and your body needs. That is 'yoga': Union of body and mind.

Whether your awareness comes about through your own awakenings, life practices or practising yoga in a class, it doesn't really matter. But that awareness and the joy that it brings is vital to your holistic wellbeing.

If you have ever experienced guilt for eating the 'wrong thing' then practising yoga, mindful awareness through any means and developing supportive eating habits will help you break the bonds of being a prisoner to your choices, feeling guilty or disempowered.

Eating what you love with some sensible rules to follow (mine include enjoying a green smoothie every day and 'adding a salad' to my meals) will make your health, life and shape change because you learn to bring conscious awareness into every part of your life.

Here's what you can put in your salads

In a word – ANYTHING!

If you happen to be reading this book because you are serious about changing your shape then I invite you to consider minimizing the amount of flesh products in your food. Start with salads. Work towards making them the main part of your meal.

I am not 'veg-evangelist' but I do know from personal experience (when I was 30 pounds heavier than I am now) that when I started listening to what my body was telling me, I gravitated towards loads more vegetables and a lot less meat and fish. It's a story I will write down for you one day for sure.

If you are trying to lose weight then my best recommendation is to learn to enjoy your salads without any meat or fish or chicken in them at all. When you do you'll feel lighter and your shape will change faster.

Eating flesh – at least for me – slows down the metabolism. and ahem, clearance of wastes. I also like the way that I can fill myself on salad and vegetables and feel light.

A note on garnishes

The very last recipes in this book are some suggestions for garnishes. Sometimes just popping something on top of your salad, guacamole, salsa, dip or sauce can just complete the picture and make it even more appetizing. It can add a crunch or help bring out particular flavors.

You will find suggestions for how to use nuts and seeds, herbs and vegetables and even a cheese-like topping that is completely dairy free. I have to admit that I love to eat this by the spoonful.

Raw and cooked recipes – but mainly raw

I believe that salads are best eaten raw. I find them way more exciting raw and I feel healthier, lighter and more satisfied as a result. This is why <u>most</u> of the ingredients in this book remain uncooked. You will find several recipes with legumes (beans) and some that have cooked grains and others that list blanched, roasted or broiled vegetables. You'll also find guidelines in those recipes to enjoy them completely raw too.

Adding meat, fish, tofu, eggs and dairy to your salads

I leave the addition of flesh products entirely up to you. If you want to add meat or fish, may I suggest preparing a per person amount and adding that portion to each plate?

You will note that I will suggest optional additions or substitutions for certain salads. Most of the time my recipes have no meat or dairy. I may mention them in a few recipes but basically, it's UP TO YOU!

If you want to add an ounce or 2 of feta, tofu, fish, chicken, beef or anything, then please feel free to do so. I am vegetarian and I eat vegan food 99% of the time. That's my confession. However, I do not push a 'barrow'. I am not trying to convince you of anything other than eating beautiful salads and dressings and dips is a cornerstone to your health.

Whatever you cook or uncook with, as the case may be, always aim to use the best possible ingredients. If you can (and your budget allows) choose organic or pesticide free (or selectively sprayed to minimize residue). Local farmers' markets are a great place to find freshly harvested produce that retains even more nutrition than the veggies you find in the supermarket.

If you were to press me for my personal opinion then I would say that to eat a diet with at least 60% raw ingredients is a healthy thing to do. To incorporate upwards of 80% raw food could even be a key to exceptional health. The internet will help you find plenty of information to support that view – both anecdotal and scientific.

Eggs

If you love eggs and want the nutrition from them then go ahead and add boiled eggs. They can add a beautiful color to your salads. Particularly if you boil them either to the point where the yolks are golden and still shiny, and just set; or keep them in just 1-2 minutes longer and set them harder. Longer again and the dark, bright golden yolk becomes pale yellow and even gets a grey tinge. So learn the cooking times that suit your taste.

If you want the nutrition of an egg yolk then you can easily add a yolk to many dressings. I don't choose to do that but it would create thicker dressings.

Tofu and Tempeh

I enjoy adding tofu and tempeh to the occasional meal. I like the texture and the flavor. What? Enjoy? Some people really don't like it at all. But please pay attention because I want to share with you a way to make it delicious.

Some people don't like the idea of eating soy products for various reasons. What you do is up to you, naturally. Here are a few facts about tofu and tempeh.

Tofu is a soy product and a good source of protein, calcium and B vitamins. It is made in a similar fashion to cheese with a coagulation process. It comes in all different varieties, firm, soft, silken and even smoked. Firm tofu is higher in calcium.

Tofu can be eaten as is or cooked in many ways. It has little inherent flavor and so it's great to absorb other flavors around it. That's how I use it, after marinating it.

Tempeh on the other hand is fermented soybeans which means it is a natural probiotic. It may even help you keep a healthy gut and immune system. It is another good protein source. Unlike tofu, in tempeh you can see the beans in the product.

Eating tempeh is one simple way to reduce your saturated fat intake, especially if you're trying to reduce or eliminate meat from your diet. It can have a good mouth feel, texture and taste.

I have to say that you may want to try different brands because I have tasted great and not-at-all good varieties.

We have a brand here called Nutrisoy that makes a very reliable and delicious organic product. It even tastes very good straight from the pack. However to transform the flavor of almost any tempeh (or tofu) you can marinate using the instructions below.

Marinating tofu or tempeh

- In a watertight sealable container put firm or smoked tofu, chopped into cubes, sliced or crumbled (I use Lock & Lock)
- Grate a generous amount of ginger over the tofu (see "A great trick with ginger")
- Grate a generous amount of garlic
- You can add spices like hot chilli pepper, or cumin and so on
- Pour over enough Bragg (or tamari) to wet (no need to drown it). Probably a few tablespoons full
- Stir if possible or just seal and turn the container over a few times to distribute. Do this a few times over the course of say, 30-60 minutes which is ideal. You can still get good results with a very short marination time of only a few minutes.

Now you can use your tofu or tempeh either uncooked, added to curries, casseroles or stir fries or lightly fried. It's a winner in our house.

A great trick with ginger

I have to credit my mummy (that's Australian for Mom) with this really brilliant tip that I have used for as long as I can remember. So, you know the problem with ginger? You buy a beautiful fresh portion and if you don't use it fairly quickly it dries out and becomes hard.

There really is nothing like the fresh tang of ginger, especially young ginger.

When you next buy ginger, keep a practical sized chunk of it accessible in the fridge or in your fruit bowl ready to use.

The rest of it, pop into a plastic sealable bag and then put it into the freezer. Yep, that's right. Freeze it.

When you need ginger, you simply take the ginger out of the freezer and grate it with a fine hand grater. So, here's the thing. Grating it without thawing creates a fine powder that dissolves. The powder actually melts giving you the fresh ginger taste. It's hands down better than dried ginger powder.

When I want the rich and full taste of ginger without my guests chewing on explosions of ginger then I go for frozen ginger. Great for children.

Oh, and when you're marinating tofu, tempeh or for that matter anything at all that needs ginger, you'll get a maximum incorporation of the ginger taste with minimum effort. Hooray!

Adding Cooked Components

The last thing before we move on to salad recipes is to consider other cooked components in your salads. Feel free to add grilled veggies, tofu, tempeh or small amounts of cooked pasta or rice. You should always greatly limit the amount of cooked food in any salad. That includes flesh products, dairy and egg. But that's just my opinion! ;)

If you crave some cooked food in your salad from time to time, simply add a handful of quinoa, rice or other grains, pasta or whatever! See if you can keep your salads 80-100% raw.

In a recent selection of weight loss recipes I advocate making traditionally hot 'main meals' by cooking a smaller component of food and adding raw vegetables prepared specially. You'll be surprised and delighted at how GREAT these taste and even more impressed with how you feel afterwards. Write to me if you would like a book based on "Raw Fusion Recipes" and then I may just write it!

The art of keeping your leafy greens crunchy and fresh (and not soggy)

Have you ever created a wonderful salad only to find that when you serve it, it's not as fresh as you wanted? Maybe the leaves went soggy.

Here's a tip from one of my lovely readers. It's a really great one! Thanks Richard. Here's what to do when you have a salad that has leafy greens or vegetables that will wilt or spoil if left too long in dressing.

Prepare your vegetables and place the harder or more hardy ones (perhaps carrot, tomato, cucumber, onion) in the bowl with your prepared dressing. Combine or toss those ingredients together.

Gently place your prepared leafy greens and sprouts on top of your veggies. Do not mix them together ... yet.

Just prior to serving, toss everything together. You'll have the beautifully infused dressing with your hardy vegetables and fresh crisp green leafies.

With this tip you'll be able to make many salads way ahead of time, allow the flavors to deepen and enhance your creations and still keep them tasting the best they can.

How To Use The Salads Ingredients Lists

You're here because you want recipes. And that's EXACTLY what I am going to give you.

At the end of the book you'll find lots of lists of ingredients that you could put in your salads. Just here you'll find a list of those lists. I really recommend you read them now because they may include ingredients you haven't used for a while. Perhaps there will be some that you have never tasted before. Maybe you'll feel excited and inspired to use them in your salads and meals from now on.

The Lists

- Tree fruit
- Citrus fruit
- Tropical and exotic
- Vegetables – Common Varieties Including Fruit That Are Considered As Vegetables
- Fruit Vegetables
- Herbs are part of the vegetable family
- Leafy and other types of vegetables
- Bulb, Root and Tuber Vegetables
- Nuts and Seeds
- Miscellaneous

Oils and Vinegars and Condiments

- Here are the oils that I use:
- Vinegars and Amino Sauces

Let's Look At Some Spectacular Salads

Remember not all of the salads here have a particular dressing to use with them. The beauty of salads is that you prepare them with a variety of ingredients in a variety of ways. THEN using this book you pair your salads with dressings from the "Dressings and Dips" section. You'll find dressings, salsas, guacamoles, toppings and dips. These are multifunctional recipes. Salsas double as salads and dressings. Dips can also be dressings.

So, yes some salads do include their own dressings. These tend to be my preferred dressing. For many salads I will give you a suggested list of dressings you will find in this book that are compatible. I will also include those salad-specific dressings in the dressings section. This will give a little repetition that will help you sort through a complete list of sauces rather than having to find 'that salad' again! It will all be in one place.

You'll also see that most of these salads are staggeringly simple and simply delicious. I hope you enjoy them as much as I enjoy eating them and sharing them with you!

A word on quantities

Some of these salads have no quantities indicated. Feel the freedom in being able to prepare the list of ingredients to suit your tastes and the number of people. There is no real number you can put on such a recipe. Mostly there will be specific guidelines.

Here's what I mean: If you are preparing food for 4 people and you are only serving 1 single salad then you'll prepare a vastly different amount to the people who are preparing 5 salads and a small conventional cooked main dish on the side.

My wish is that you'll have your own little salad revolution at your house. Enjoy the bounty of tastes and relish every mouthful.

Happy eating!

~ • ~

The Salad Recipes

~ • ~

~ • ~

1. Simply Zucchini

For the 'first cab off the rank' I want to start with something special and especially simple.

I am not kidding when I say this is one of my favorite salads EVER. You'll be surprised at how simple it is. The other thing that surprises me is that you can start with a heaped pile of raw undressed zucchini (or summer squash), you add the dressing and 3 minutes later it appears to be about a third of its volume.

Generally if I am making this salad for 2 I would spiral 1.5 of this elongated fruit (regular size about 6 inches and moderate size).

Salad

- Spiral grated zucchini

5 minutes before you serve your meal add your super simple dressing.

Dressing

- Squirt on some Bragg Liquid Aminos (a tablespoon for the amount mentioned above)
- Drizzle some sesame oil over the top (toasted makes the sesame taste stronger)
- Stir to incorporate and then let sit for a few minutes

There! I told you it was simple.

Alternative dressing (although nothing beats the one above)

- Lemon juice
- Olive oil
- A little sea salt

Options & variations

For a different mouth-feel use a hand peeler or a mandolin to slice beautifully long ribbons of zucchini. Curls of ribbon look very decorative on the plate.

~ • ~

2. Radish, Asparagus and Mushroom Salad

I love asparagus. Here it is here with mushrooms and radishes in a well-balanced dish that will please just about everyone. My favorite café has a similar salad from which I was inspired to pen this recipe.

Use the asparagus raw, or blanched for 30 seconds, or steamed for a couple of minutes.

Rather than cut the asparagus into 2 inch sections (which is very common) you'll slice these ones diagonally very finely so that you can enjoy the real taste in every mouthful.

- 1/3 cup red radishes, sliced finely in semilunar pieces
- 1/2 pound (1/4 kilo) asparagus, cut off the fibrous end, sliced diagonally, finely
- 1/2 pound (1/4 kilo) mushrooms, cleaned, sliced finely
- 3 cups watercress sprigs

Dressing recommendations

- 2 tbsp fresh lemon juice (1.5 for metric chefs!)
- 2 tsp white wine vinegar
- 2.5 teaspoons Dijon mustard
- 1/2 teaspoon salt
- 1/3 cup olive oil
- freshly ground black pepper

Garnish

- 1/3 cup "Surprise Me Cheesy Sprinkles"
- 1 green onion or 1/4 cup chives, finely chopped

Assemble the salad ingredients in a bowl. Whisk the dressing and adjust your seasonings. It needs to pack a little punch! Remember, that if you find the dressing too acidic, add a touch of agave or honey.

After tossing the salad, top with the sprinkles and your greenery!

~ • ~

3. Fenn-tacular Salad

I must say I really love this salad. It is spec- ... no! It's fenn-tacular. Surprising and tasty. A lovely mix of flavors and textures. And, it seems to go with a myriad of dressings. The amounts here are very good for a good sized lunch or a side salad to share. Scale up as you need to.

Salad

- 1 cup fennel finely sliced
- 1 pear, sliced finely
- 1 orange, supreme cut (see below, remove membrane of the segments)
- 2 tbsp walnuts or pecans, crumbled for good size and mouth feel
- Optional, highly recommended: A tbsp. or 2 of capers or a handful of olives (remove the pits and chop them)

I think it always goes without saying but just in case you need the reminder, grind on some sea salt and pepper to taste.

Options and variations

To make this a more substantial salad then add a couple of cups of green leaves. I love rocket, tatsoi, watercress or spinach for this salad.

Dressings recommendations

Consider the "Orange Ginger Vinaigrette", or a citrus-based dressing.

I have tried this particular salad with many different dressings. From "Dollop Sweet Cream" plain, the same cream with pepper and spices, with minced fresh ginger! I have had it with "Spiced Apricot Vinaigrette" "Mang-nificence" and plain vinaigrettes such as one with just lemon juice, olive and salt. All good.

Preparing the orange (to 'supreme')

To supreme the orange means to remove the segments from the pith. The best way to do this is to 'top and tail' the orange and then peel it with a knife. The blade takes the peel and the very outside of the pith from the fruit itself.

Now hold the orange in your hand over a bowl (or place it on a chopping board). Place the blade just inside the pith of the segment to separate flesh from white pith. Place the blade down the other side of the segment and as you do, the bit of orange will be set free!

Eventually you'll be left with a wheel of the pith (and a little orange in there that you didn't access.

Since your hand is already wet and orangey squeeze all the remaining juice either into the salad you're preparing, or into a dressing. I can usually manage to harvest about 1-2 tablespoons of juice.

~ • ~

A note about grated vegetables

How you grate your veggies really affects how they taste. Sounds odd. My least preferred type of grater for hard and firm vegetables such as carrot, pumpkin, zucchini (etc) is the garden variety upright grater. Prepare the same vegetable in different ways and feel and TASTE the difference.

The grater on the left is a classic grater. On the right is just one variety of spiral grater.

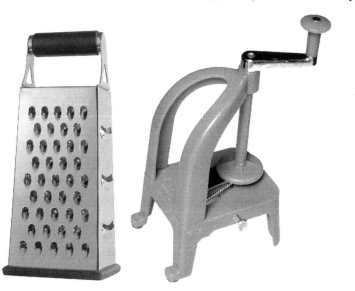

My newest favorite toy is the Tefal Fresh Express. Although (unfortunately) it does not spiral-grate, the whole family really loves the feel of the different sized grated pieces.

While this machine doesn't appear to be available (under that name at least) in the US, it does get mixed reviews. We really like it a lot. Spiral graters to look at (again, our preference) are the Benriner and the Lurch. See what your food processor can do.

A note about SPIRAL-grated vegetables

Sometimes, and particularly when you have different varieties of spiral-grated vegetables in the same bowl, the strands can be long. If they are VERY long it could make it more difficult to portion the right amount of salad or 'spaghetti' on your fork.

It could also make it a little challenging to combine and distribute the different colors and tastes equally throughout your dish.

What I do is grate my vegetables, place them on my chopping board and then cut through the middle of the mass of the vegetable once or twice.

Then everything combines well and separates more easily when you're serving and eating your lovingly created dish!

~ • ~

4a. Carrot Salad

Carrot salad keeps very well over a number of days. In fact, it's one salad that you can add the dressing to and it seems to get better every day. I always make quite a big amount of it. If I am going to the effort of spiraling the carrots then it is definitely worth it to me to grate another 3-6 carrots.

The dressing recipe that immediately follows is for a small amount of carrot salad (say, perhaps 3 medium carrots).

Salad

- Spiral carrots (not grate). It will be just like spaghetti. It coils beautifully on your plate and on your fork. It's a pleasure to eat it this way rather than grated in the regular way. The shape that the vegetable becomes when spiral-grated and how it feels under the tooth does rather surprisingly, have a major effect on the way you experience the taste.

Dressing

- 2 tbsp oil of choice (olive, coconut, walnut, avocado or other)
- 1 tbsp vinegar (apple cider or even coconut vinegar or other)
- 1 tsp of mustard (Dijon or other mild mustard)
- Sea salt
- 1-2 cloves garlic, crushed or minced (start with 1)
- Cracked or ground fresh pepper

Whisk in a bowl. Or add dressing ingredients to a jar. Close the jar and then combine.

Taste and adjust your seasonings. Depending on the strength and type of vinegar and mustard used you may need to add more.

Dressing recommendations

To really complement the carrots it really wants the sour or acid flavor of the vinegar and mustard. If you find you've added too much vinegar (and that happens) then balance it with a splash of agave or honey (or other liquid sweetener). I promise that works! When you taste it, remember it needs to be strong-ish because the flavors dilute when you add dressing to salad. Feel free to add more mustard or vinegar. Try "Spiced Apricot Vinaigrette" or experiment with any other vinaigrette or non-creamy dressing.

4b. Carrot Salad Variations

You can add anything you like to your carrot salad. Try these:

- Sultanas (raisins)
- Basil
- Cilantro (coriander)
- What about spiralized zucchini
- Handful dried coconut
- Pistachios
- Cranberries
- Olives

~ • ~

5. Thai Green Papaya Salad

Colorful, crunchy, tasty.

Just as in "Asian Spiced Papaya Salad", wear gloves if peeling your own green papaya. One of my local vendors in the farmers' market has green papaya already grated in a bag. How convenient and lucky. I just go home and start chopping the other ingredients.

Using the Bragg Liquid Aminos gives this salad a very Thai flavor. You'll love it.

Spice it up by adding 1-2 finely chopped chilli peppers. Thai green or red chillies work well.

Salad

- 1 medium green papaya, peeled, deseeded and grated or julienned or spiraled
- 1 cup red bell pepper (capsicum) finely sliced into strips
- 1 carrot, julienned
- 1 cup bean shoots (sprouts)
- 1/2 red (or brown) onion, sliced
- Optional other crunchy and colorful ingredients: Try jicama, celery, zucchini
- Add nuts or seeds, peanuts if you eat them, walnuts, pecans, sunflower seeds etc
- 2 tbsp herbs, finely chopped. Choose any or all: Cilantro, mint and basil

Dressing

Thai Tamarind Dressing

- 2 tbsp Bragg Liquid Aminos (add more as desired)
- 1.5 tbsp sesame oil
- 1 tsp tamarind paste if you have it
- 1 tsp coconut palm or rapadura or other sugar
- 1-2 tbsp lime juice, add extra to taste
- 1/4 tsp sea salt
- 1/4 tsp freshly ground black pepper

Place the papaya, carrot and all other chosen vegetable ingredients in a bowl. Whisk all the dressing ingredients together in a small bowl or shake them up in a jar. Now add the dressing to the salad bowl and toss the salad.

Taste test your salad and add extra Bragg, lime, sugar or sesame oil to taste. Just as you would in any salad or dressing!

Garnish

- 1/2 cup cilantro, chopped
- I also like sliced to garnish with chopped stalks of green (spring) onion

Serve!

~ • ~

6. Indian Kachumber Salad

Do you love Indian food? We love it at our house. When our daughter is out, we tend to spice up our curries. Kachumber can be, but doesn't actually have to be spicy. That is always up to the cook and the diners. It is a popular dish of limitless varieties that is served on the side.

Basically you start with tomatoes, onions, salt, sugar and lemon. Then you add other ingredients to vary. Cucumber is often added.

Robert and I just love freshly minced ginger on our tomatoes. Then we garnish with fresh ground black pepper.

Salad

- 3 tomatoes sliced fine or diced. Up to you and the texture you're after
- 1/2 red onion, halved and then finely sliced
- 2 tbsp lime juice
- 2 tbsp cilantro, chopped
- 1/4 cup finely chopped green onion
- 1/4 tsp cumin powder
- 1/2 tsp ginger, minced
- 1/8 tsp cayenne pepper
- 1/4 tsp sea salt
- Top with freshly ground pepper

Combine and then serve.

~ • ~

7. Pineapple Curry Salad

Salad

- 1 cup pineapple, diced
- 1 red onion, diced, or in fine slices
- 1 cup green beans, diagonally sliced
- Optional: Rocket or mixed leaves

Line a bowl with leaves, top with your dressed salad.

Dressing recommendations

Dress pineapple, onion and green beans with "Spiced Apricot Vinaigrette"

Options and variations

Cut 2 cups of rocket leaves small and toss with the pineapple mix and the vinaigrette.

~ • ~

8a. Tomato Salad

I sometimes get frustrated with complex recipes. The delight of having several salads at the table lends itself perfectly to having a couple of very simple dishes along with a more elaborate one. Fresh tasty tomatoes with basil, onion and a simple dressing is hard to beat.

Salad

- 4 fresh firm tomatoes diced
- 1 onion diced
- Optional: Generous amounts of basil sliced

Dressing recommendations

Any dressing. 'Dip' in and find something that takes your fancy. Try these suggestions:

- A simple drizzle of extra virgin olive oil over the tomatoes, with sea salt and either lemon juice or apple cider vinegar
- "Basil Basic"
- "Mang-nificence"
- "Black Olive Dressing"

Options and variations

- Slice your tomatoes into 1/4 inch rings.
- Slice your onion finely.
- On a serving plate place a tomato and onion slice and then a basil leaf. Continue to work your way around the plate so that there is overlap and they join up at full circle.
- Drizzle oil, sprinkle with sea salt and pepper.
- Powder the plate with "Mineral Sprinkles" and pop a sprig or 2 of basil in the center for decoration.

8b. Summer Tomato Salad

The addition of nectarine (or mango not both) in summer makes this one of the most delicious salads you will ever eat. Tear or slice your basil leaves to be fairly large rather than what you would do for a regular tomato salad.

Salad

- 2 tomatoes cut in wedges (more attractive) or sliced
- 1/2 small red onion, sliced in rings or long strips
- 1/4 cup basil, torn or sliced in strips
- 1/2 mango or 1 nectarine, cubed

Combine the salad, add a dressing and gently toss.

Dressing recommendations

Use a vinaigrette of your choice. Or just splash on some olive oil, lemon or lime juice, some sea salt and freshly cracked pepper. Mmmmm...

8c. Tomato Salad Variations

A couple of suggestions to vary your tomato salads.

- Cucumber
- Feta (if I am going to eat cheese, which I do rarely, I eat an organic feta)
- Or smoked tofu
- Or your choice of meat or fish

Garnish

- Dust on some black pepper
- We like the zing of fresh minced ginger
- Dust with "Tomato Powder" or "Surprise Me Cheesy Sprinkles"

~ • ~

9. Waldorf Salad

Salad

- 1 stalk celery finely sliced
- 2 apples diced
- 1/2 cup walnuts, chopped
- 1/2 small onion diced
- 1/2 medium red bell pepper (capsicum) diced or sliced
- Optional: A lovely touch is adding 1/2 cup dried raisins (or sultanas)
- Optional: Some halved seedless grapes

Dressing recommendations

The classic thing with a Waldorf Salad is to dress it with a creamy dressing. So many to choose from you could use "Creamy Garlicky Sauce", "Blond Lemon", or for a fantastic culinary adventure try the "Peppered Spicy Dollop Cream".

~ • ~

10. It's Rocket Science

Simplicity is beautiful. Try a simple rocket only salad. Or add the other ingredients. Add a dressing and you're done.

Rocket is one of my favorite leafy greens. As one of the several salads on the table purely and simply by itself will provide an excellent difference. Here I have added certain ingredients to embellish a plain leafy salad.

Salad

Amounts are per person for a good meal-sized portion:

- 1.5-2 cups rocket (arugula, roquette – however you spell or say it)
- 2 tsp pine nuts
- Some fine onion slices
- 1 tbsp chopped sundried or 1/2 medium fresh tomato, sliced, chopped or in wedges
- 1-2 sliced dried figs

Dressing recommendations

The spiciness and crispiness of the leaves, nuts and onion lend themselves to a vinaigrette. Dip in and make a choice.

I would also recommend "Tomango Dressing", "Mang-nificence" and "Balsamic Vinaigrette".

If you fancy a creamy dressing dollop on some hummus, some "Kinda Sorta Sour Crème", a simple "Guacamole" or any you discover (!) even over your already vinaigrette-coated salad.

~ • ~

11. Sweet & Sour Cucumber Salad

This little Asian-inspired wonder has a sweet and sour palate. Another family favorite. For best results use a mandolin. If not make sure you use a sharp knife for even slicing. I created a dressing that I call my "Sweet and Sour Sesame Asian Dressing".

This salad keeps very well for several days and benefits from marinating in the dressing too. If you find you have a lot of cucumbers on hand then prepare them all. Then you can adjust the dressing recipe to match. I prefer soft skinned cucumbers that are not bitter and require no peeling.

Salad

- Finely slice your cucumber
- I actually prefer this one with just cucumber. But you can optionally add some finely chopped onion.

Dressing

Sweet and Sour Asian Dressing:

Try this first using 1 or 2 tablespoons as your 'part'. Scale up from there when you have large quantity of cucumbers to process.

- 1 part oil of choice, I use sesame oil (it's milder tasting when it's not toasted)
- 2 parts apple cider vinegar
- 1 part raw honey (my preference) or other sweetener (agave)
- Sea salt
- Pepper to taste
- Optional pinch of cayenne pepper

What you're after is a slightly sweet yet tangy sauce! It's best to taste test this one as you're preparing it.

~ • ~

12. Sweet and Sour Cucumber Salad Mark II

Take 2 with this very different and very worthy variation of my cucumber salad. Instead of liquid sweetener you'll have the sweetness from the apple and fruit, balanced with the citrus (on the apple, in the dressing and served alongside).

Salad

- 1 red crispy apple, diced, immediately coated with a tbsp lemon juice to stop it going brown. Do this first and set aside
- 2 cups of cucumber, finely sliced into rounds or half rounds
- 2 tbsp dried cranberries OR raisins OR 3 dates diced small
- 1/4 cup pecans, chopped

Prepare the apple. Then prepare the cucumber, cranberries, nuts in a bowl.

Dressing

- 2 small chilli peppers sliced finely
- 2 tbsp olive oil
- 1 tbsp lime juice
- Sea salt and pepper to taste

Whisk the oil, chilli, salt, pepper and lime juice together. Dress your salad.

Garnish

- Lime or lemon, sliced into wedges for 1-2 per serving. Looks great on the communal platter and on each plate. Your diners are in control of the level of citrus.
- Sprinkle with 1 tbsp finely chopped dill
- Or dust with sesame seeds (black and or white)

~ • ~

13a. Glass Noodle Salad

Glass noodles are very fine transparent rice noodles which you cook. There's not much to them. They take on the flavors that you add. They have a pleasing feel under the tooth. So ...   for the same effect but with more nutrition substitute kelp noodles. See the next recipe.

~ • ~

13b. Kelp Noodle Salad

This is an amazingly delicious meal or side salad with an Asian twist! You'll love how easy it is to prepare and how great it smells and looks as well. It is well worth the trouble to get hold of these nutrient-rich kelp noodles.

If you haven't any kelp noodles on hand then use rice or other noodles. It's up to you.

Don't worry if you don't have all the herbs available. I do recommend at least including 2 of the herbs. You are after the aromatic taste sensation that the combination of herbs brings.

Your noodle pack will tell you to soak the kelp first. I have found that the noodles soften perfectly in the dressing without adding another step to the process. You can separate the strands over the course of a couple of minutes when they're wet.

Salad

- 1 packet of kelp noodles
- 1 handful of mint, very finely chopped
- 1 handful of basil leaves also very finely chopped
- 1 handful of cilantro or coriander very finely chopped
- 1-2 julienned carrots (cut like matchsticks, use a mandolin, a knife(!) or a julienne hand grater – mine looks just like a peeler with teeth on it, or a machine like the Tefal Fresh Express)
- 1/2 julienned red pepper (capsicum)
- Finely sliced red onion (or white or shallots)
- Tofu (in strips, or grated and then marinated in Bragg, ginger, garlic) 3oz or 100g
- 10 halved cherry tomatoes

Dressing recommendations

- Coconut milk or coconut cream, about 1/3 to 1/2 a tin
- A dash or 2 of Bragg liquid aminos (or tamari or soy if you haven't got Bragg which has a more delicate and less overpowering flavor)
- 1 garlic clove grated or crushed
- A good squeeze of lime or lemon juice
- A little sea salt
- Optional: A sprinkle of dulse (wonderful mineral profile)
- Optional: 1/2 teaspoon or more of grated ginger

If you have a jar of "Siam Sesame Dressing" in the fridge then consider using it with to top your salad or in place of the above dressing.

Garnish

- Garnish with coarsely chopped cilantro leaves

Options and variations

Another great nutritious condiment is coconut aminos. I love them because they are delicious and sufficiently different to Bragg and tamari to create a little culinary drama and interest!

Add nuts, sprouts, julienned zucchini, anything that inspires you to put more vegetables, crunchy texture and color into your salad.

~ • ~

14. Coleslaw

A simple salad that is versatile with many different tastes depending on the dressing. This salad is classically eaten with a creamy dressing. In this book there are many creamy AND healthily delicious dressings from which to choose.

But there's nothing stopping you choosing something lighter. Check out the "Dressings" recipes for ideas.

Coleslaw generally keeps well. Classic dressings that are based on 'real' mayonnaise will last longer than creamy dressings based on nuts and other ingredients that you will find in this book. So keep in mind that for the sake of freshness and optimum flavors consume this salad within 2 days and 3 at tops!

My personal preference for most salads – except my favorite and fabulous carrot salad – is to compile dressing and salad for the meal that I am eating. I would prefer in most cases to keep extra quantities separate and unmixed. This gives me way more flexibility.

I get different taste sensations by mixing and matching to my heart's desire. That way nothing tastes like a leftover!

Salad

See proportions below

- Cabbage finely shredded both red and white
- Onion finely chopped
- Carrot cut in fine matchsticks or grated
- Sesame seeds

A good rule of thumb in this salad is to use 2 cups of cabbage to every 1/2 chopped onion, 1/2 cup julienned or grated carrot and 2 tablespoons of sesame seeds.

A beautiful option is to add caraway seeds to your slaw. For every 2 cups of cabbage (see previous paragraph) add 1 teaspoon of caraway. They have a very distinctive flavor.

Dressing recommendations

Choose a (creamy) dressing from the next chapter. Here are a few ideas for you. Don't limit yourself to just these:

- "Kinda Sorta Sour Crème"
- "Lemon Cashew"
- "Sweet Mustard Sauce"
- "Minted Pear"
- "Mangorient"

~ • ~

15. Sweet Slaw

Salad

- Use the same formula for your basic slaw as in the recipe above.
- 2 cups cabbage finely shredded both red and white
- 1/2 cup onion finely chopped
- 1/2 cup carrot cut in fine matchsticks or grated
- 2 tbsp sesame seeds
- Add 4-5 thinly sliced dried apricots
- Add 1/4 cup raisins or dried cranberries
- Add 1/4 tsp powdered cinnamon (or if you like nutmeg or allspice then use them)

Dressing recommendations

You guessed it a creamy dressing is great with this. But that should never stop you 'shopping around' for a light clear dressing. Perhaps "Spiced Apricot Vinaigrette".

I can highly recommend "Variations 4 & 5" of the "Sweet Dollop Cream" recipe.

- Complement the sweetness with "Creamy Garlicky Sauce".
- Try "Blond Lemon" or even "Silky Minted Pear".
- Try the Aioli or one of the Caesar dressings".

~ • ~

16. Kaleslaw

Colorful dark green and bright red and orange slaw. A delight for the eyes too!

Salad

- 2 cups shredded kale, no stalks, stacked leaves, tightly rolled up and sliced finely
- 1 cup red bell pepper, finely sliced
- 1 cup carrot cut in fine matchsticks or grated
- 2 tbsp sunflower seeds

Garnish

What's really pretty is to layer some long thin slices of avocado over the top of your platter or individually served plates of salad.

Dressing recommendations

- Prepare the slaw ingredients. Add a mayonnaise style dressing. Try the "Mustard-Almond Aioli" one of the "Caesar" dressings, and "Sweet and Sour Asian Dressing".

~ • ~

17. Crunchy Slaw

Salad

I can't always find jicama where I live. It has such a pleasing crunch. So even if you can't find it there are plenty of other crunchy morsels in this list of ingredients. It's the preparation that counts and creates the right consistency.

- 1 cup white cabbage
- 1 cup red cabbage
- 1 cup jicama julienned
- 1 green apple julienne grated
- 1 cup red pepper, finely sliced
- 1 medium carrot in sticks
- 1 medium onion (red or brown) sliced finely

Options and variations

- Add 1/2 cup cranberries or dried raisins/sultanas
- Another colorful addition that gives a pleasing crunch: Add the corn kernels from an ear of corn

Dressing recommendations

Slaws usually partner up with a creamy dressing. Because they are sweet in nature go for balance with a dressing that will provide a touch of citrus or vinegar.

- The usual suspects are "Blond Lemon", "Sour Crème", "Lemon Cashew" "Mango Avocado".

~ • ~

18. Nuts Over Broccoli

A sea of green trees and a splash of color and crunch.

A very versatile recipe where you decide whether to steam, blanch or prepare your broccoli raw. Amazingly, raw broccoli, if the florets are small and bite-sized, will take on a softened partly cooked type of consistency if it sits in the dressing for about an hour before serving. It's part of the marinating process.

Salad

- 2 cups broccoli, cut florets into bite sizes (or smaller)
- 1/2 medium onion chopped or sliced
- 1/3 cup raisins
- 1/2 cup diced red pepper
- 1/3 cup pine nuts

Add your vinaigrette style dressing to at least your broccoli making sure it is well turned to coat all surfaces for about an hour. Let it sit in the fridge .

Or take your cooled (steamed or blanched) broccoli and coat it in your chosen dressing. Add other ingredients and serve your salad.

Blanching

Blanching involves boiling water with a touch of sea salt. Put your broccoli in, bring it back to the boil and leave in for a minute. Then remove and 'shock' in cold water. It will have pleasingly softened while maintaining a vibrant green color.

Dressing recommendations

"Honey Spice Vinaigrette" and "Tomango Dressing" are quite adventurous and delicious with this. Go the straight and narrow with a 'normal' vinaigrette and it will be equally delicious.

~ • ~

19. Mushroom Salad

Raw mushrooms. Some people love them and others ... not! You can enjoy the soft, cooked appeal of mushrooms or the crunchy or firm texture depending on the dressing that you add.

You can prepare all the mushroom recipes in this book with raw, lightly sautéed or seasoned roasted mushrooms.

Mushrooms take on flavors easily. Marinating them in a light dressing will soften them beautifully as you'll discover with this recipe.

Use button, field or any mushroom of choice. With any mushroom you should clean it by wiping it with a clean tea towel.

Washing mushrooms should be avoided because it makes them somewhat waterlogged because of their structure.

Salad

- 1 pound or 1/2 kg of mushrooms, cleaned, finely sliced
- 1/3 cup parsley, chopped
- Optional: Add green beans and green onion

Dressing recommendations

You can do something as quick as splashing on:

- Equal amounts of lemon juice and olive oil
- With some sea salt and pepper

Or, go crazy and pick out a daring vinaigrette:

- "Lemon Ginger Sesame Sauce", "Lemon Ginger Vinaigrette" comes to mind. For traditional try "White Wine Vinaigrette"
- Maybe even "Honey Spice Vinaigrette" which has a mild sweetness.

For creamy dressings try:

- "Blond Lemon Dressing"
- Add "Creamy Garlicky Sauce"

Options and variations

For a decadent finish, mushrooms pair wonderfully with truffle oil. Use an uncomplicated dressing in that case.

Other ideas:

- Add chives
- Add slightly spicy greens such as rocket or watercress
- Add green beans.
- Green beans and mushrooms seem to go together very well. Either keep the beans raw or blanch them.

20. Mushroom, Citrus and Spinach Salad

- 1/2 pound (250g) mushrooms
- 1 small red onion, halved and then sliced
- 1 medium orange, supreme cut (pith removed)
- 1/4 cup pine nuts
- 1/4 cup cranberries (craisins)
- 1/2 tsp tarragon, fresh finely chopped, or dried

Dressing recommendations

"Orange Ginger Vinaigrette", an orange based "Easy & Delicious".

Or try this:

Orange vinaigrette

- 1/4 cup orange juice
- 2 tbsp lime juice (metric users start with 1.5)
- 1/3 cup olive oil
- 1.5 tbsp agave or honey
- 1/4 tsp sea salt
- Fresh black pepper (I add 1/4 tsp but you add to taste)

Whisk in a bowl. Adjust the acidity with extra lime if needed, or balance with honey and oil.

21. Kale Salad

Even though this salad has a dressing within its recipe listing, you can embellish it beautifully with a big dollop of guacamole or salsa or luscious dip, decoratively placed on your platter or individual servings.

The first time I made a raw kale salad cutting it finely and 'massaging' these lovely leaves with the dressing, I was pleasantly surprised at how much like steamed kale it was. I was so pleased I had found a way to preserve the nutrients by not cooking my greens.

What's more, my young daughter loved making and eating it too.

Salad

Firstly

- Bunch of kale, sliced finely (see below for 'chiffonnade' instructions)
- 2 tbsp extra virgin olive oil
- 2 tbsp fresh lemon juice

Then add

- 1 red pepper (capsicum) diced
- 1/2 tsp salt
- Freshly ground black pepper to taste
- 3 tablespoons raw pine nuts
- Optional: A handful of either sliced black olives or sultanas

Enjoy your salad!

You may want to add more dressing or dollop a thicker style one on top as well. Think salsa, dip, or guacamole.

Chiffonnade

- Wash your kale carefully.
- Cut or tear the stalks out.
- Line the leaves up on top of each other and roll them up tightly into a cylinder shape.

- Now start to cut very fine ribbons off the end of the cylinder and put them in a bowl.
- Pour the oil and lemon juice over the kale and use one hand to massage the dressing into the kale for about 30 seconds. Wait a couple of minutes and then massage again for 30 seconds.

You will notice after a couple of 'massaging sessions' that the kale will wilt and soften in the same way it would if you were to steam it. The passage of time will also help the dressing soften the leaves.

Options and variations

- Use Swiss chard, or other large leaf greens instead of kale
- Use Bragg and sesame oil instead of olive oil and lemon juice.

~ • ~

22. Watermelon and Red Onion Salad

Decades ago I was at a Christmas lunch with my then boyfriend (whose name was also Robert!). On the table was a salad that I had my doubts about. But after tasting it, I can honestly say that this one should not be missed.

Choose a ripe, crisp-fleshed watermelon. I am very particular with this fruit. I actually like to buy one that's already cut. That way I can make sure that the pink color is 'just right'. Bright red flesh to me usually means floury and soft. Choose clear pink with tight cells.

Seedless watermelon is obviously something that you can aim for but you know what? If you find a beautiful melon and it has seeds, either work around them or eat them! The seeds have a very good mineral profile.

Also feel free to add other ingredients. See the list of suggestions below. Here's what you put in the basic rendition:

Salad

- 3 cups watermelon flesh, diced to slightly bigger than 1/2 inch cubes (2 cm if you are metric-minded)
- 1 small red onion finely sliced
- Black pepper, freshly ground, to taste
- Optional: Add 2 cups of spinach, rocket or watercress sprigs

Dressing recommendations

You can dress this one with a simple vinaigrette of your choice. Start with a 'garden variety' basic with olive oil and vinegar or citrus juice. Graduate to the more adventurous ones.

Options and variations

- Add 1/4 mint, washed and then finely chopped
- For a complementary crunch add 1 stalk of celery, finely sliced
- Add a handful of black olives, pitted and sliced

~ • ~

23. Steamed Salads

You can lightly steam your vegetables. Oh, OK, some of them need a good steaming to make them palatable and stop them being so hard: Potatoes or sweet potatoes, for example. Actually, sweet potato is rather lovely raw when you grate it, combine it with other vegetables and a great dressing.

But the types of vegetables that you can have either soft or lightly steamed include Brussels sprouts, carrot, onion. Me, I really cannot bear mushy mooshy broccoli. For me, it has to have a crunch and that vibrant green color. If it's overcooked it's soft and unpalatable.

When you're steaming your veggies, place them in, in stages. First the potatoes and sweet potatoes and onions (and possibly carrots if you like them very soft). Then after 10 minutes place in carrots(!) and pumpkin. Another 5-10 minutes add Brussels sprouts, broccoli, asparagus, corn and so on.

To preserve the shape of your pumpkin pieces, keep the skin on. Pumpkin may be hard raw but becomes mushy if you steam it too long.

Once you turn off the stove or steamer and you are setting the table or have just 2 minutes left before serving, think about popping in a handful of snowpeas or fine zucchini slices. Certainly put in your bok and pak choy, chard or waterspinach at this stage.

You will enjoy different textures. Enjoy mashing some things and crunching on others.

Dressing recommendations

- Add any of the dressings from the supplied recipes: Either a favorite from some of the salads, or any of the "Dressings".
- One of my personal (and family) favorites for steamed vegetables is "That Tahina Dressing" which is based on tahini.

Final note! Serve with a salad – the cold variety. If you've got some creamy style dressings with the hot dish, then use a vinaigrette style dressed salad. Say, a spiralized carrot salad and or a green leafy salad and you're done!

~ • ~

24. Super Salad

Another Scanlon Family Favorite. You can put *anything* and everything in these salads. The trick is to choose an accent so that you can repeat your salad or, alternatively you can create a new one every time!

Please see the section at the beginning of the book called "Making Super Salads".

Salad

- Cut up everything you love so it's nice and small
- Grate anything from sweet potato, to carrot to zucchini, use different graters but make the pieces small
- Red pepper finely diced
- Onion, finely diced
- Cut up fresh mango or nectarine, apple, dried apricot or fig
- Add corn kernels, chopped tomatoes, avocado, olives, cucumber
- Add pumpkin seeds, sesame seeds, sunflower seeds
- Use herbs like basil, mint, dill and coriander
- Add some tempeh, tofu or smoked tofu
- Enjoy cheese? Then crumble some feta in there

The flavors of all the different ingredients combine to create something VERY tasty. We often don't even put a dressing on it at all.

Dressing recommendations

Anything at all. You could use ANYTHING from this book. You will develop favorites.

I have been known to blend up a mango and avocado and a little sea salt or Bragg and just drizzle that on. Or just my "Easy & Delicious" or "Basic Vinaigrette". When you create delicious and nutritious dressings then you can have several different taste sensations at the table at the one time just to go with the one 'naked' salad.

Try "Mang-nificence". Try "Lemon Cashew 1 or 2". Try "Rich Tomato Dressing", "Moroccan Dressing". Try anything!

~ • ~

25. Pesky Peach & Pecan

I love peaches. Peaches are in season for such a short time (relatively speaking) so don't limit yourself to making this just a summer salad. If you don't have fresh peaches on hand, plump up some dried ones to soften them and release the flavor and then slice them.

Use any lettuce really! But what honestly sets off the peach very beautifully is a couple of tablespoons of basil. Or mint.

Salad

- 3 medium ripe peaches, yellow or white flesh
- 3 cups rocket leaves
- 1/3 cup pecans, halve the halves to keep them looking attractive
- 1 green onion, chopped finely
- Sea salt and freshly ground black pepper
- 2 tsp capers (or for a sweeter touch, a handful of craisins or raisins)
- 2 tbsp basil OR mint finely sliced

A good quality feta with a nice salty note complements the sweetness. If you add feta use 1/4 cup crumbled or cubed.

Dressing recommendations

You have carte blanche with this salad. So many citrus based vinaigrettes lift this salad. Perhaps it will be your favorite too.

Try "Orange Ginger Vinaigrette", "Thai Satay" for something very different. Or "Lemon Cashew Dressing", "Basil Basic", "Lemon Ginger Sesame Dressing", "Spiced Apricot" or any "Easy & Delicious" dressing.

~ • ~

26. Zesty Chickpea Salad

Smoked tofu or feta goes well with this salad, so please yourself and just add it in, in 1/3 inch or 1cm cubes.

Salad

- 1 regular sized tin of chickpeas (garbanzo beans), drained
- 1/2 cup cherry tomatoes halved
- 2 cups rocket (arugula)
- 1/2 small onion, diced

Dressing

- Zest of one lemon (1/2 to 1 tsp adds the right zing) and then ...
- 2 tbsp lemon juice
- 3 tbsp fresh basil, chopped small
- 3 tbsp fresh parsley, chopped small
- 4-5 tsp olive oil
- 1 clove garlic, minced
- 1/4 tsp ground salt

So simple to prepare. Whisk the dressing ingredients in a bowl. Then just add everything and toss to distribute the herbed dressing. Add your garnish.

Alternatively, blend your dressing.

Garnish

Any or all of the following:

- Sprinkle with freshly ground pepper
- Add some sliced avocado
- Add some sprigs of herbs
- Add a dollop of a thick dressing, cream, guacamole or salsa.

~ • ~

27. Fennel Salad

The flavor of fennel is fresh and aromatic. For many it is an acquired taste. Taste a little to see how strong it is. It has a decidedly aniseed accent. It marries well with rocket and crunch from other ingredients. If you're unsure then start with 1/2 cup of fennel.

Salad

- 1.5 cup fennel bulb, finely sliced
- 1 large green apple, (julienned) cut into match sticks or thin slices
- 1 cup mixed greens or arugula (rocket)
- 1 tbsp fresh finely chopped thyme (or tarragon)
- Optional: 1 tbsp chilli pepper, seeded and finely minced or some cayenne or paprika

Combine all ingredients together. If you have to prepare this before you are ready to eat, then add some dressing or plain lemon juice to the apple to prevent it going brown.

Dressing recommendations

- Try serving with "Easy & Delicious" dressing with a tablespoon of lemon zest and a clove of crushed garlic if desired.
- Just about any citrus vinaigrette or fruity dressing is a winner with this salad.

~ • ~

28. Cucumber Tomato Dill Salad

Salad

- 1 cucumber, chopped into chunks or fine slices
- 1 cup tomato, chopped
- 2 tablespoons scallions, or 1/2 onion chopped
- 1 cup sorrel
- 1/4 cup dill, then finely chopped
- 1 handful sesame seeds or sunflower seeds

Options and variations

- For a different zesty experience use watercress or endive.
- For mild leaves choose romaine or spinach leaves

Dressing recommendations

Add your desired dressing. I enjoy a vinaigrette or adding simple lemon juice, salt and pepper with or without olive oil.

~ • ~

29. Zucchini Pasta Salad

Pasta salads can be served warm or cold. They can be cooked or raw too. If you love conventionally cooked pasta then use 2 cups of cooked small shapes of your choice. Otherwise ribbon slice some zucchini (see below for instruction) for an equally delicious and somewhat fresher experience.

Salad

- 2-3 zucchini, ribbon-sliced with a peeler or mandolin (and then chopped to make 'pasta lengths of 2-3 inches (5-10cm). See below
- OR instead of zucchini ribbons use 2 cups cooked pasta shapes of your choice
- 1/2 onion, sliced finely
- 3 large tomatoes, diced fairly large
- 2 tbsp small capers
- 1/4 cup basil leaves, finely sliced
- 1/2 cup parsley leaves chopped

Garnish

Optional garnishes include:

- "Surprise Me Cheesy Sprinkles" (are non-dairy, taste like parmesan and divine)
- Parmesan cheese, grated
- Chopped "Homemade Semi-Dried Tomatoes"
- Sunflower seeds

Zucchini preparation

Prepare the zucchini ribbons and onion and place in a bowl. Sprinkle a teaspoon of sea salt all over, toss to distribute and then let sit for about 10 minutes. Excess water collects in the bottom of the dish in this process. Drain this liquid. Pat your zucchini ribbons dry. Cut your ribbons into small lengths. Assemble your salad.

Dressing recommendations

Choose a dressing or vinaigrette determined by your desire at that moment. Simple olive oil and salt and a splash of Bragg (the same as in "Simply Zucchini") pairs well..

Recommended recipes from this book include:

- "Basil Basic"
- "Lemon Ginger Sesame Dressing"
- "Mustard-Almond Aioli"
- "Lemon Cashew Dressing"
- Caesar Dressings or Guacamoles

~ • ~

30. Wild Herb Salad

Go crazy adding different leaves and herbs then add olives, onions, tomatoes and avocados. I tend to make my salads from the best available seasonal ingredients. So even with the best intentions, sometimes I can't make an exact recipe because an ingredient or 2 are simply not around that week! If an ingredient is not available you could substitute something for it. If you find an ingredient that's not in a recipe, that shouldn't stop you from using it either. The joy of food preparation is flexibility, fun and featuring different tastes, colors and textures.

Salad

- 1/2 cup arugula
- 1/2 cup romaine lettuce
- 1/2 cup red leaf lettuce
- 2 cups of fresh herb leaves including basil, cilantro, parsley and mint (a little rosemary)
- 1/2 red onion sliced
- 1/2 medium cucumber finely sliced
- 1 carrot, finely sliced
- 1/2 cup red bell pepper, matchstick sliced
- 1 big tomato, chopped
- 3 sundried tomatoes, sliced or 1/4 cup "Homemade Semi-Dried Tomato" wedges
- 6-8 olives, pitted (add whole or sliced)
- 2 tsp sesame seeds
- 2 avocados, halved and sliced into wedges
- 1 orange supreme cut (instructions below)

Prepare your salad with everything except the avocado and orange. Fold half the avocado and orange when you combine your salad and dressing. Then arrange the rest of the fruit on the top of your salad.

Garnish

Consider a sprinkle with seaweed powder for a little extra nutritive burst, some seeds or nuts.

'Supreme' cutting your orange

The most attractive way to present orange segments in a salad is to 'supreme' them. Instead of peeling the orange, 'top and tail' the fruit, then cut the skin off just taking off the outside of the pith. This reveals the bright orange cells of the fruit.

Cradle the orange in your hand and with a knife, remove each segment with 2 careful cuts just inside the pith.

Dressing

Try this salad with "Easy & Delicious" Or "Lemon Ginger Sesame Dressing" or use the "Sesame Vinaigrette Dressing" just below.

Sesame Vinaigrette Dressing

- 2 ½ tbsp cold pressed olive oil
- 1 tsp raw sesame tahini
- 1 tbsp lemon juice
- 2 tsp Braggs Apple Cider Vinegar
- 1 garlic clove, minced
- Sea salt, to taste

~ • ~

31. Breakfast Fruit Salad

Enjoy the bounty of a cornucopia of fresh fruit. Remember you can create very quick nutritious meals with fruit (and greens). Add herbs like mint to fruit and you have an even better combination.

The quantities below will suit 2-4 people depending on what else is being served. One very hungry person could spend a morning eating this as their breakfast over a couple of hours.

Salad

- 1 cup fresh strawberries, quartered
- 1/2 cup fresh blueberries
- 1/2 cup fresh pineapple cut in chunks
- 1/2 cup watermelon cubes
- 1/2 cup cantaloupe or honeydew melon in cubes
- 1 kiwi fruit, sliced
- 1 cup grapes
- 1 peach, diced
- 1/2 pear, chopped
- 1/2 mango, chopped
- Optionally add a handful or 2 of green leafy vegetables. They combine very well with fruit.

Either combine all the fruits together or layer them in a bowl for a lovely visual effect!

Options and variations

Optional: 1 banana, sliced (if you're eating your salad straight away then add a banana. If not it will turn brown, so cut it and add it last thing before serving).

See next page for Dressing recommendations.

Dressing recommendations

While this salad doesn't need a dressing, try this with a fruit and avocado dressing or a mango dressing. "Mang-nificence" is sweet and tangy with some optional chilli.

Even the one with cumin that follows it "Cumin Scented Mang-nificence". "Mango and Avocado" is more savory with garlic notes. "Orange Chipotle" is worth a try. What about something creamy?

Try one of the "Dollop Sweet Cream" variations, or "Minted Pear Silk". Here is a list of vinaigrettes you may like to try: "Raspberry", "Lemon-Ginger", and "Orange Ginger". And even with a sweet/savory garlic hint: "Sweet Ginger Sauce" or "Lemon Ginger Sesame Sauce". Phew.

~ • ~

32. Minty Grape Salad

Without or with a dressing ... simple, easy, yum.

Salad

- 1/2 pound or 250 g of green grapes sliced or chopped
- 1/4 cup shredded fresh mint
- Combine and let sit for the flavors to combine before serving.

Options and variations

- Substitute pineapple instead if you like
- You can even serve this on a bed of greens with a dash of balsamic vinegar
- Dress this one if you wish.

~ • ~

33. Potato Salad

Mostly when I make salads it's because I want raw vegetables. But sometimes, just sometimes I add cooked ingredients. Potato salad is very popular with guests. It's very versatile too. It pairs well with vinaigrettes but even better with creamy dressings, aiolis and mayonnaises.

The soft potato marries well with chewy dried fruit, crunchy celery and green onion. The largely light color of potato is the perfect blank slate or palette for beautiful colorful vegetables.

Salad

- Steam 2 good sized potatoes, cooked, cooled, cubed
- 1/4 cup red pepper, diced
- 1 stalk celery, sliced finely
- 1 green onion, sliced diagonally (keep half for garnish)
- 2 tbsp sunflower seeds
- 1/4 cup parsley, chopped
- 1/2 cup corn kernels

Options and variations

- Dried apricot diced small, or cranberries.
- Nuts or seeds for crunch

Remember potato types have different mouth feel. Some will be waxy and firm, others will be more soft when cooked. You may want one that keeps its shape more easily.

Dressing recommendation

Any dressing!

~ • ~

34. Peppery Pear & Walnut Salad

It's the pepperiness of the green leaves that just goes so well with the sweet of the pear and crunch of the nuts. Either drizzle olive oil and lemon juice with a generous sprinkling of sea salt and pepper, or choose a dressing. See recommendation below.

Salad

- 1/2 cup of pear (with or without the skin), sliced or cubed
- 1 cup of rocket, chopped
- 1 cup of watercress, chopped
- 2 tbsp walnuts, chopped

Options and variations

- Finely slice a few radishes

Dressing recommendations

- Enjoy the simplicity of "Easy & Delicious" (olive oil and lemon juice, salt and pepper)
- Or try a dollop of "Rawquefort Blue Uncheese Dressing" which is salty, pungent and complements this sweet peppery salad.
- "Minted Pear Silk" works.

~ • ~

35. Celeriac Salad

I don't see celeriac very often where I live. We lived in France for half a year back in 2005. You can buy a delicious celeriac salad in the supermarkets. It's superb with a creamy dressing. So, I made up my own based on this French classic.

Celeriacs are fascinating to look at. They are a root vegetable and you will find them in all sorts of tortuous shapes. When you prepare them you will most likely find that a lot of it ends up trimmed off because of all the soil entrapped. Once you get to your clean trimmed vegetable, grate it with a machine or hand or spiral grater.

Salad

- 1 celeriac, cleaned, trimmed and then grated

Options and variations

If you want extra crunch with a very complementary flavor, finely chop or grate some celery too. They are cousins you know!

Dressing recommendations

Add a creamy dressing. One that has some sour acid notes with some mustard or vinegar, and some pepper, balanced by some sweetness.

- Try "Kinda Sorta Sour Crème"
- "Mustard-Almond Aioli"
- "Lemon Cashew" Dressings 1 and 2
- "Blond Lemon"

~ • ~

36. Avocado Grapefruit Salad

Preparing your grapefruit can be done by adding the segments or by a technique described below called to 'supreme'. Taking the extra time to supreme your citrus will not only make your fruit far more attractive, the bitter pith will be gone, so you will enjoy a better tasting creation.

Salad

- 4 cups lettuce of your choice
- 1 grapefruit, segmented or supreme, see below
- 2 avocados cubed
- 1 cup of diced cucumber
- 10-12 cherry tomatoes, cut in half
- 1 small red onion diced
- 1 red bell pepper diced
- 1 red, orange or yellow bell pepper diced
- 1/4 cup cilantro chopped
- Optional and recommended: 2 tbsp diced "Homemade Semi-Dried Tomatoes"

Combine the above ingredients in a bowl and add dressing.

Or arrange leaves on a platter or on individual plates, Dress the salad and arrange on the leaves.

Preparing the grapefruit (to 'supreme')

To supreme the grapefruit means to remove the segments from the pith. Chop off the peel (and pith) from the top and the bottom of the fruit. Now peel it with a knife including removing the pith just under the peel.

Now hold the fruit in your hand, over a bowl. Place the blade down each side of the segment and as you do, the bit of grapefruit will be set free!

Since your hand is already wet squeeze all the remaining juice either into the salad you're preparing, or into a dressing.

Dressing recommendations

As you have quite a lot of avocado in this salad I recommend choosing something light. "Easy & Delicious". "Robert's Favorite", "Honey Spice" "Dijon Tarragon" or any other vinaigrette.

~ • ~

37. Minty Orange Salad

No need to dress this salad. If you supreme the oranges you will squeeze the juice (that is waiting in the pithy remains) right over the bowl. This will allow all the ingredients to mingle beautifully.

Salad

- 3 oranges
- 1 tbsp (or more) of shredded fresh mint
- 2 tsp of peeled finely grated ginger

Combine and let sit for the flavors to combine before serving.

Preparing the orange (to 'supreme')

Slice off the top and bottom to reveal the fruit. Place the fruit down to peel it with a knife, removing the pith just under the peel as you sweep the knife down in a curve.

I find it easier to hold the fruit in the hand, over a bowl. But you could put it on a cutting board. Place the blade down each side of the segment and as you do, the bit of orange portion will come away!

Since your hand is already wet, squeeze all the remaining juice either into the salad you're preparing, or into a dressing.

~ • ~

38. Greek Salad

Just like any salad, this one can be a meal in itself. Greek salads are typically made with big chunks of vegetables. If you like a stronger garlic accent to your salad, optionally add a finely sliced clove of garlic. Great for taste and mouth feel.

Salad

- 2-3 cups romaine (cos) lettuce or other mild green leafy, torn into bite-sized pieces
- 1 cucumber, sliced (not too thin, you want to feel a crunch)
- 1/2 pound of cherry tomatoes, halved
- Or chop 2-3 big tomatoes into wedges
- 1 red bell pepper, chopped or sliced
- 1 small red or white onion, sliced and separated into rings
- 1 big handful kalamata olives
- Add sea salt and cracked pepper to taste

Options and variations

Add any or all of the following to the ingredients above:

- 1 handful of radishes, sliced finely
- 1/2 cup chopped parsley
- 1/4 – 1/2 pound (100-200g) crumbled or cubed feta cheese
- Substitute marinated tofu for feta cheese

You can either combine this salad in a bowl or arrange it on a large plate!

Garnish

- Sprinkle with 2 teaspoons dried oregano

Dressing recommendations

Dress with "Easy & Delicious" dressing (or just have the sauce at the table in a bowl or serving jug). Vinaigrettes pair well.

~ • ~

39. Tabouli Tabbouleh Tabbouli

... whichever way you spell it, it's a classic.

Salad

- Soak cracked wheat for 1 cup yield
- OR if you're eating more raw food, sprout some quinoa or buckwheat
- 1 big bunch of parsley (about 2 cups) very finely chopped
- 1 big bunch of mint, very finely chopped
- 3 large tomatoes, diced
- 1 medium cucumber, diced
- 1/2 red onion diced
- Optional: Zest of 1 lemon

Dressing recommendations

Use the dressing of your choice. For a classic tabbouli taste choose:

- "Easy & Delicious"
- "Basic Vinaigrette".

Options and variations

You can use this on nori sheets spread first with "Avocado Salad" above. Roll it up just like sushi! Mmmmm... ☺

Some raw foodists actually finely chop cauliflower (processing it in a machine so it's small and crumbly) instead of using wheat or sprouts.

~ • ~

40. Asian Spiced Green Papaya Salad

One of those supremely healthy dishes. Papaya (or pawpaw) aids digestion because of its enzymes. Peeling papaya is a sticky business so wear gloves. The results are definitely worth the effort. Your papaya must be green!

Salad

- 1 medium green papaya, peeled, deseeded and grated. I cut chunks and spiralize because the texture is really pleasing (or use my electric grater to julienne)
- 1 carrot, spiraled or grated
- 1/2 cucumber sliced in strips
- Nuts such as crushed macadamia, some pine nuts, peanuts, or walnuts
- Herbs of your choice, 2 tbsp of each (basil, mint, coriander, parsley, dill)
- Other ingredients for color and crunch. Optionally add: Green beans, bean sprouts, other crunchy colorful vegetables such as snowpeas, bell peppers, jicama

Place the papaya, carrot and cucumber and any optional ingredients in a bowl and drizzle the dressing over the vegetables. Combine to coat the contents of the bowl in the sauce.

Serve on a platter and garnish with the seeds and cilantro.

Garnish

- 1 tbsp (black?) sesame seeds, for garnish
- 1/2 cup cilantro, for garnish

Dressing recommendations

Use the dressing ingredients here. Or use "Siam Sesame Dressing".

Coconut Lime Spice Dressing

Dial back on the spice (cayenne and chilli pepper) if you need to

- 3 tbsp coconut milk
- 2 tbsp lime or lemon juice
- 1 tbsp sesame oil
- 1 tsp honey, or agave or maple syrup
- 1/2 tsp ground cardamom
- 1/3 tsp cayenne powder
- 1/2 tsp sea salt
- 1/3 tsp freshly ground black pepper
- 1-2 finely chopped red chilli pepper
- 1 tsp cumin powder

In a mixing bowl, whisk together all the dressing ingredients. Check flavor and add components if necessary

~ • ~

41. Ripe Papaya Salad

This salad combines the sweet yet mild flavor of papaya (pawpaw) with that of the stronger and more spicy greens. If you like very strong greens then go for endive. I have suggested rocket or watercress. The dressing that works so well with this simple salad is based on lemon juice. For an extra zing, add some jalapeno or perhaps a Thai chilli pepper.

Salad

- 2 cups of ripe papaya, peeled and cubed
- 3 cups of green leafy vegetables, chopped as you wish.

Dressing

- 3 tbsp lemon juice, freshly squeezed
- 2 tbsp extra virgin olive oil
- Sea salt and black pepper to taste. Try 1/4 tsp of each
- 2 tsp of jalapeno or other chilli pepper

Place salad ingredients in a bowl. Whisk dressing ingredients together and add to your salad.

Options and variations

- Substitute milder greens (such as tatsoi and spinach) instead of the endive, watercress and rocket if you prefer.
- Add in other colorful vegetables. Some green onion. Jicama. ...

~ • ~

42. Green Bean Salad

Easy to make. Easy to pair with any dressing, vinaigrette, thick, creamy, salsa or guacamole. Or throw over some sesame oil and Bragg Liquid Aminos and be done!

Salad

- 1/4 pound or 100 g green beans (raw or blanched) cut into 2 inch lengths (5cm)
- 1 small red onion, halved, then sliced for semi-lunar shapes
- 1 cup rocket leaves
- 1/2 cup red bell pepper, diced
- 1/4 cup cranberries (craisins)
- Optional: 2 tbsp chopped pecans or walnuts

Dressing recommendations:

Vinaigrettes work well. Try:

- "Balsamic Vinaigrette"
- "Orange Ginger"
- "Lemon Ginger Sesame Sauce"
- Or just a plain "Easy & Delicious" with a dollop of "Blond Lemon Dressing".

Dip into this book choose … just about anything!

~ • ~

43. Chickpea Salad

What makes this salad shine is choosing a tasty dressing. The textures of the quinoa, chickpeas and leaves are juxtaposed by the corn, radish, cucumber and onion (and other chosen crunchy candidates!).

I like to use canned chickpeas. Yes I know, you could start from scratch and soak and cook your own, but honestly, my schedule sometimes just doesn't always allow for the 'slow food' approach. However, when I do have the time this salad is just perfect for substituting in sprouted chickpeas.

Add in anywhere from 1.5-3 cups of cooked quinoa to make this a more filling hybrid (cooked/raw) salad.

- Prepare 1 cup of dried quinoa so you have about 3 cups on hand. You will need 2 cups water (or stock) for cooking the quinoa (salt the water and put a dash of olive oil). Full instructions at the bottom of this recipe.

Salad

- 1.5 - 3 cups cooked quinoa (see instructions)
- 3 cups spinach leaves or arugula or watercress torn or cut into shreds
- 1 tin chickpeas, drained
- 1 medium carrot, julienned grated
- 1/2 cup red onion, diced

- 1/2 cup cucumber, diced
- 1/3 cup parsley, chopped
- 1/4 cup red radishes halved and then finely sliced
- 1 handful of snowpeas, cut into 1/4 inch diagonal slices
- 1 ear corn, shucked
- 1/4 tsp sea salt
- 1 garlic clove minced
- Optional: Handful of black olives
- Optional: 1/4 cup sunflower seeds OR chopped hazelnuts

Dressing recommendations

Decide which dressing style you like and then smother your salad. You could choose any salsa. I love the "Kinda Sorta Sour Crème". And I love "Siam Sesame Dressing". I could equally enjoy it with "Blond Lemon" or any Vinaigrette. Your hardest job is choosing!

Cooking the quinoa

Soak the quinoa for 5-10 minutes to soften it. Now rinse abundantly until the water is completely clear, to get rid of the 'saponins'. Drain it very well. Bring 2 cups of water (with or without flavoring with stock) to the boil. Add the quinoa. Allow to simmer for 10 minutes with the lid on and the heat turned down. Then turn the heat off, remove the pan halfway off the heat and let sit for another 10 minutes. You MUST leave the lid on the whole time or the cooking process will be hampered.

Loosen the quinoa with a fork. It must not be wet. Leave the lid off and allow the quinoa to cool. Stir through the vegetables and the chickpeas. Fold through the leaves. Add your dressing. Serve.

~ • ~

44. Crunchy Jicama Salad

Jicama is not something I find a lot of where I live (in Australia). But when I do I snap it right up because the family really enjoys the crunchy texture. Isabelle loves munching on coated 'raw' fried 'chips'. Everyone loves it. Because it does not have a strong flavor, it really is a matter of 'what you do with it' that counts.

With this salad try either to chop it into matchsticks OR process it more into little bits to resemble corn kernels or even cous cous grains. Processing your veggies differently even makes your salad taste change.

Peel the jicama by breaking the skin and pulling back the brown layer. It separates very easily.

To follow this recipe you will find two processing options within the brackets. The first for a more textured salad with larger pieces; the second for more of a cous cous style salad.

Salad

- 1.5 cups jicama (matchsticks or processed, see above)
- 1/2 small red onion (sliced or diced)
- 1/2 cup red (pepper) capsicum (matchsticks or small dice)
- 1/2 cup cilantro, chopped
- 1 ear of corn, shucked
- Optional: Red chilli pepper, minced

Dressing recommendations

Choose any salad dressing: Classic, Asian inspired, Light, Thick, or Creamy.

~ • ~

45. Seaweed Salad

Seaweeds and their preparation

Seaweed is an excellent way to nourish yourself. You'll find 2 seaweed salad recipes right here. In addition, towards the end of this book you'll find a chapter called "Garnishes and Snacks". There you'll find 2 recipes which are wonderful seaweed based recipes to garnish and season just about any salad, salsa or dip. These are the "Mineral Sprinkles" and "Mineral Sesame Sprinkles" recipes.

This book would not be complete without a seaweed salad. In my books (that's author speak for 'in my opinion') the best seaweeds to include in a salad are arame (ah-rah-may), hijiki and wakame (wah-kah-may). To prepare your seaweed you will firstly soak it in warm water. This softens it. Depending on which variety it could take 10 minutes or 30 minutes.

Drain your seaweed and squeeze out excess water. While arame and hijiki grow in thin strips wakame may come to you as wider strips. You may want to trim it to size. Experiment with the different sea vegetables to see which one you prefer. This recipe you can use one type of seaweed, or create a mix of all three (or other favorite varieties not mentioned here).

Salad

- 2 cups seaweed (using 1-3 varieties as mentioned above)
- 1/2 cup cucumber, julienned
- 1 cup red pepper in matchsticks
- 1/2 small onion, finely sliced
- Sesame seeds to garnish. White and or black.

Place in a bowl, combine with a dressing and then garnish with sesame seeds.

Dressing recommendations

- "Sweet Ginger Sauce" with some minced red chilli pepper.
- "Siam Sesame Dressing"
- "Sesame Vinaigrette"
- "Sweet and Sour Sesame Asian Dressing"
- "Thai Satay Dressing"

~ • ~

46. Bountiful Seaweed Salad

With the addition of some green papaya or even green mango you will enjoy the play of sweet and sour and the crunch of the salad. Adding leafy greens and the fruit makes this a more substantial dish - even a main.

Salad

- 2 cups seaweed (using 1-3 varieties as mentioned above)
- 1/2 cup cucumber, julienned
- 1 cup red pepper in matchsticks
- 1/2 small onion, finely sliced
- 2 cups of green leafy vegetables
- 1 cup of green papaya, spiral or julienne grated
- 1 medium carrot, peeled, cut in matchsticks
- 1/2 beet, peeled, cut in matchsticks
- Optional: 1-2 small red chilli peppers, deseeded, minced

Prepare the green papaya and squirt with a little Bragg Liquid Aminos before adding to the rest of the salad. You can use tamari, soy sauce or coconut aminos.

Combine all ingredients except your garnishes. Top with your sesame seeds or Mineral Sesame Sprinkles.

Dressing recommendations

- "Sweet Ginger Sauce"
- "Siam Sesame Dressing"
- "Sweet and Sour Sesame Asian Dressing"
- "Thai Satay Dressing"

Garnish

- Top with Gomasio ("Mineral Sesame Sprinkles")
- Chopped cilantro
- Or both chopped cilantro and sprinkles

~ • ~

47. Rainbow Salad

Ever thought of just processing your vegetables and NOT tossing them? For a beautiful layered appearance that's different from your average salad, you can choose a rainbow of vegetables, slice and grate them onto a platter or into a bowl, garnish with herbs, and serve alongside a jug of dressing. Voilà. Hey, why not create several dressings?

Salad

Prepare a selection of colorful vegetables and layer them onto your plate as you make them. Choose one cut or different ways to create textures between layers.

- Zucchini
- Carrot (orange or purple or both)
- Fennel
- Sweet potato
- Red onion
- Celeriac
- Radish
- Red pepper
- Green or yellow beans

That's just a small list. Go to "The Lists Of Salad Ingredients" for more inspiration.

Dressing recommendations

A blank palette allows you to choose anything

Garnish

Top with nuts, seeds or dried fruit if you like.

~ • ~

Sixteen Different Salad Ideas

Here are some ideas for you. No amounts just small collections of ingredients. Embellish them with toppings, herbs, garnishes. And choose your dressing, salsa or dip.

Corn kernels, snow peas, red onion

- Great topped with sesame seeds

Rocket, grated beetroot, orange segments

- Peel the orange segments (supreme them) it's more beautiful and tastes and feels better in the mouth

Zucchini, crumbled cauliflower and cranberries

- Different textures make for an interesting experience.

Carrot spirals, mung bean sprouts, zucchini matchsticks

Avocado, spinach leaves, orange segments

Chickweed (or watercress), peach and sunflower seeds

Pineapple, endive and red bell pepper

Rocket, fresh or dried figs and apple

- Lime and orange juice

Jicama sticks, carrot and red bell pepper

Dried apricot, orange or yellow bell pepper and carrot

Beet, watercress, avocado and grapefruit

Red onion, nectarine, basil and tomato

Endive, pear, green apple

Rocket, walnuts, nectarines, red onion

Cucumber, tomato, onion

- Cucumber and tomato in equal amounts and same size small cubes. Needs a good amount of sea salt.

Strawberries, almond, spinach

~ • ~

48. Roast Pumpkin And White Bean Salad

There is something so utterly enticing about roast pumpkin. The sweetness of grilled or roast pumpkin is alluring, nutty and soft at once. Pairing it with greens, beans and pine nuts is a match made in heaven.

Roasting or grilling this orange fruit with its skin on helps hold the flesh together. I love to eat the skin. Oh, I believe that in the US and Canada that you use the word broil for grilling in your kitchen oven. That is not in use in Australia. We just call it grilling whether it's outside at the barbecue or in the kitchen.

While I have included a vinaigrette recipe below, you can substitute it for any other dressing you wish.

Roasting or broiling your pumpkin

You will have to roast, grill or broil your pumpkin first and then assemble your salad.

- 2 lbs or 1 kg of pumpkin (your choice) chopped into cubes (3/4" or 2 cm cubes) OR cut long slices of about 1/4" thick (that's less than a cm)
- Brush the pumpkin with olive oil, sprinkle with sea salt and a little cracked pepper
- Optionally add a sprinkle of dried herbs
- Place the pumpkin on baking paper or on a non-stick baking tray

To roast:

- Place in a preheated oven at 360°F (180°C) for 25 minutes turning at least once. The pieces will become tender and change color.

To grill (ok, broil):

- Place under a hot grill. Keep an eye on these to avoid burning Check every 5 minutes. As the broiler and the food heats up, you will have to check at shorter intervals.

Salad

- The prepared pumpkin (from instructions above)
- 1 cup cannellini beans (from a tin is fine)
- 2 tbsp pine nuts
- 2-3 cups rocket
- 1 cup cilantro, chopped

Dressing

Mild Chilli Bragg Vinaigrette

- 1/4 cup olive oil
- 1 tbsp Bragg Liquid Aminos (or Tamari, or soy, nama shoyu)
- 1 red chilli pepper, deseeded if required, and chopped
- 2 tsp honey or agave syrup
- 1 small clove garlic, minced
- 1/4 tsp sea salt

Whisk the dressing ingredients together in a bowl. Taste test and adjust seasonings. Add some lemon juice or vinegar if you need a little more acid balance. Add the pumpkin, rocket, beans, cilantro and pine nuts and the cilantro (reserving a small amount of cilantro for garnish).

Garnish

With coriander (the rest of the cilantro).

~ • ~

49. Pear, Watercress, Hazelnut, Beetroot, Dried Fig

Beetroot or beet, is just beautiful as a raw vegetable (spiral or julienne grated) or in chunks that you broil or roast. So with this salad no matter how you like your food, cooked or uncooked, dairy or vegan you will love this salad.

And by the way, if you can come up with a better name for this salad, please let me know! I actually like reading the ingredients in the title and couldn't think of anything more evocative of the tastes and textures. So do contact me.

Salad

- If you're spiral grating your beetroot then just grate 1 beet
- If roasting or broiling use 1-2 beets cut into chunks, use scant oil and some sea salt
- 2 cups or so of ripe, crunchy pears (your choice), cut into matchsticks
- 1/4 cup of hazelnuts (raw, or even dry roasted in a pan) chopped roughly
- 3 cups watercress sprigs
- 3 dried figs finely sliced
- Optional: Goat's cheese or any   feta , sliced

Dressing

Honey Spice Vinaigrette

- 1/4 cup olive, walnut or hazelnut oil
- 1 tbsp red wine vinegar
- 1/4 tsp sea salt
- A good grinding of fresh pepper
- 1/4 tsp cinnamon
- 1/4 tsp cumin
- 1 tsp honey

Whisk all the dressing ingredients and then combine with the salad ingredients.

Options and variations

Don't like or eat cheese but want that flavor reminiscence? Dollop some "Kinda Sorta Sour Crème" and or sprinkle some "Surprise Me Cheesy Sprinkles".

~ • ~

50. Carrot, Orange, and Ginger Salad

Carrots are one of the easiest ingredients to find. Here's a way to dress them up (simply) for a very pleasing and simple dish. The sweetness of the carrot and orange and maple syrup is complemented by the ginger and watercress. Add the crunch of pistachios and you're done. The amounts here would be sufficient for a shared salad, or a good sized single serving for a light lunch.

Salad

- 3 medium carrots, spiral or julienned, or even very finely sliced round discs
- 3 cups of watercress
- 1/3 cup unsalted, shelled pistachios
- Optional (recommended): A handful of dried raisins or craisins (cranberries)

Dressing

- 3 tsp of maple syrup
- 2 tbsp olive or avocado oil
- 1 tsp fresh minced ginger
- Optional (recommended): 1/2 tsp or more of orange zest
- 2 tbsp fresh orange juice
- 1/4 tsp sea salt and cracked pepper to taste

Prepare the carrots and leaves. In your salad bowl whisk together the oil, maple syrup, ginger, zest and juice. Season with salt and pepper. Add your prepared carrots, leaves, nuts and dried fruit directly to that bowl and serve.

~ • ~

Salsas, Guacamoles And Sour Crème

~ • ~

~ • ~

51. Simple Avocado Salad

Is it a dressing, a salad, or a dip? Actually it's all three. It all depends on the consistency.

You can dice, roughly mash (or smash) the avocado which works well for salads. Or you can mash it well or even blend it to make a dip or sauces. The texture differences are important and make each variation feel and even taste different.

This ridiculously down-to-earth recipe is really 'the simplest of guacamoles' with its 2 ingredients. I have included 6 guacamole variations in this book in addition to this one here - obviously with more ingredients!

The simplicity of this recipe is obvious. So obvious that perhaps most people would neglect to do it. Miss out on this family favorite at your peril. Thin it down with a little water (or avocado oil) if you like. Or just dollop it on!

Salad

- Mash avocado
- Add generous amounts of sea salt

Garnish

Use anything you like (or leave it 'au naturel').

Garnish with a range of different ingredients to change the look, taste and appeal.

- Top with chopped chives, cilantro, parsley or basil
- For a beautiful contrasting red try paprika, sweet, smoked or spicy
- Sprinkle with cumin or coriander powder
- Dust on some paprika or cayenne
- Add some "Mineral Sesame Sprinkles"
- Sprinkle some sunflower or sesame seeds
- Simply drizzle some vibrantly green avocado oil
- Grind some fresh black or green or red peppercorns

Serve!

So now you have the basics, read on for the variations.

If you don't finish this one at your meal then in order to store it you will need to add lemon or lime juice and combine it thoroughly. Me? I just eat the last couple of mouthfuls.

Mixing through some other ingredients creates different guacamoles. So let's take a look at some of those!

~ • ~

Guacamole Rules!

Play with the consistencies of your guacamoles. Mashing is easy and instant. Try also cubing your avocado instead. You may very well enjoy the consistency.

Any guacamole can be served in many ways. Classically, serve it with tortilla chips. If you're a raw foodie then make dehydrated chips. Dip pieces of vegetables in for a dish that is pretty much universally loved.

The sort of vegetables ('crudités') you could enjoy include snowpeas and celery, carrot and zucchini ,bell peppers, baby corn, radishes and jicama.

Where to start, what to add

Above we started with avocado and salt. That's your most basic (and arguably the most delicious) of all guacamoles ... at least for avocado aficionados. So don't feel obliged to add anything else.

From there you add lime juice (or lemon). Then some cilantro or coriander, some onion, some heat (chilli peppers) and maybe tomato.

And from there you can get very creative. Add Mexican inspired spices, onion, cucumber, herbs, dried fruit and more.

Chilli peppers

Chilli peppers add in flavor not just heat. You will choose the appropriate chilli pepper depending on your taste, your 'audience' and your wishes for your dish. These include your classic Mexican food additions: chipotle, jalapeno and serrano peppers. You may have to settle for a Thai chilli, a habanero (they're hot) or whatever your market sells.

Some chillis come in tins or jars. These are useful. Some chillis can be found dried too. You would soak them in a little water and can even use the soak water.

Just as with any produce, the quality and the heat can differ from fruit to fruit. Don't assume that the spiciness is identical to the last fruit you used.

Sometimes you need to play it safe

While you're testing the waters of any recipe or chilli, add half of what is recommended. Taste test the heat of your dish and then add more so that you don't overdo it.

If I know a chilli is very hot I will wear a glove on one hand and use the knife in the other. From experience too, make sure your hands, the knife and board and any chilli specific implements are well cleaned. The spiciness may accidentally transfer to a dish or mouth of an unintended recipient! Believe me, it happens.

If you are careful handling the chilli with a gloved hand and cut with another (and you could even wash the blade of your knife with your gloved hand) then you will have minimized most risk. If you don't use a glove then don't touch your eyes or nose for some time after as you may be sorry you did.

Adding tomatoes

Two general rules:

- For best results for consistency, appearance and taste, deseed your toms.

- Combine with your guacamole just before serving to guard the best consistency.

Storing guacamole

Guacamole is best prepared just before you need it. Use the next hint (plastic wrap) if you need to make it ahead of time.

If you actually have some left over (!) then cover with some plastic wrap that you can press onto the surface. The grey brown color that occurs is due to the avocado oxidizing. So cover it. And/or you can add lime or lemon juice.

Avocados (and simple guacamoles with no tomato etc) can be stored frozen but you have to remove the skin and pits and then blend the flesh with lemon or lime. Put it in a sealable plastic bag and squeeze out the air.

Sour cream

Although I do not mention it often, feel free to add sour cream if that's your desire. If you want something that's even creamier than avocado and you want to avoid dairy then make yourself a portion of my "Kinda Sorta Sour Crème". You'll find it among the guacamole recipes and again in the dressings and dips section. I base my sour crème on soaked pine nuts (or soaked cashews if I don't have any pine nuts available). You'll get the extra creaminess, the sour note and you will actually fool many of your guests. I know I have!

~ • ~

52. Simple Guacamole

- Avocado mashed with a fork, or chopped into little cubes
- 1-2 tablespoons green (spring) onion or red onion chopped fine
- Lime juice to taste
- Sea salt

Combine. Serve!

~ • ~

53. Smoky Guacamole

The smoky taste for this guacamole comes from the smoked chilli pepper. Jalapenos that are smoked are called chipotle chillis. I love them! You can buy them dried or prepared in jars or tins. A very popular preparation is chipotle in adobo sauce.

Chillis vary in strength from fruit to fruit, dried to tinned. So unless you know the impact of any chilli in a recipe, err on adding less. You can always add, add, add.

- 2 tomatoes, chopped and seeded
- 1/2 red onion, chopped
- 2 avocados, flesh only
- 1 small-medium clove garlic minced
- 1 chipotle chilli, either dried and soaked or one from a tin (start with half and then add more)
- 1/4 cup cilantro, chopped, 2 tsp reserved for garnish
- Optionally add 1/2 tsp red or green chilli finely chopped

If you need a little 'bite' without the hot spiciness of the extra chilli add some fresh lemon or lime juice for balance. Just a teaspoon at a time.

The great thing about this smoky guacamole is that if for some reason you have a dip that is too spicy, simply add more avocado.

~ • ~

54. Tomato Guacamole

Most of the ingredients in this guacamole are what one could consider to be a classic tomato based guacamole. I love to add my own "Homemade Semi-Dried Tomatoes" for a rich intense tomato flavor in addition to some fresh toms.

- 2 avocados mashed or cubed
- 1 med-large tomato, deseeded and diced
- 2 tbsp chopped semi-dried tomatoes (homemade or store-bought)
- 1 small red onion (or 1/2 medium) diced
- 1 tsp cumin powder
- 1 clove garlic, crushed or minced
- 1 tbsp finely chopped fresh chives
- 2 tbsp finely chopped cilantro (coriander)
- 2-3 tsp fresh lime juice
- 1/4 tsp sea salt (and more to taste)
- A pinch of cayenne pepper, chipotle powder or smoked paprika (to taste)

Combine all ingredients.

~ • ~

55. Corny Cumin Guacamole

- 1 ear corn, shucked
- 2 avocados, mashed or cubed
- 1/2 small red onion, chopped
- 2-4 tbsp fresh lime/lemon juice (start at 2 tbsp especially metric users, and work upwards in teaspoons)
- 1/2 tsp cumin powder
- 1/2 tsp fresh chopped chilli or a chipotle (rehydrated or from a can)
- 1 small garlic clove, minced
- Optional: Add a deseeded chopped tomato

Garnish

Sour cream or my "Kinda Sorta Sour Crème" is optional. A dollop in the middle and garnished with herbs and paprika is very delicious.

~ • ~

56. Lazy Salsa Guacamole

- Mash or cube 2 avocados
- 3-4 tbsp of any delicious salsa from this book or use your favorite store-bought salsa.

There, I told you it was easy!

~ • ~

57. Kinda Sorta Sour Crème

True story: My mom was over for lunch and I prepared this mock sour cream. I offered to give her some to take home. She said that although it was one of her favorite dressings that she would prefer not to have anything dairy. I giggled and told her that there actually is no dairy in it! She did take me up on my offer by the way, and took ALL my sour crème home!

The recipe will make something semi-fluid. That's perfect for use as a dressing. If you want to use this as a dollop crème, one that you can place say, on top of a salad, a guacamole or salsa, then add 1/4 (to 1/3) cup of avocado and then blend again until smooth.

This will create a wonderfully thick sour crème that will hold its own. I don't like to add too much avocado otherwise the color changes and it ends up being a guacamole. About 1/4 cup works really well.

- 1 cup pine nuts (soaked for 1 hour, drained)
- 1/2 tsp sea salt
- 1 clove garlic chopped
- 1 tsp agave syrup or honey
- 3 tbsp lemon juice
- 1/2 cup water

Blend it, baby! Make it smooth.

Taste test it. You may choose to add more lemon or salt. Remember to add 1/4 cup avocado if you want a dollop consistency.

Options and variations

Stir through some minced fresh herbs. Use cashews if you have no pine nuts. Personally I prefer the crème with pine nuts.

~ • ~

58. Grapefruit Guacamole Salsa

Ruby red grapefruit are the ones of choice for this salsa. The color really sets off the green of the avocado, especially if you supreme it. Use whatever color grapefruit you find.

- 1/4 cup red onion, diced
- 1 large grapefruit, supreme** & chopped
- Flesh of 1 or 2 large avocadoes, cubed
- 1/4 cup cilantro, chopped
- 1 tbsp olive oil
- 1 tsp agave nectar
- 1 small garlic clove, minced
- 1 tbsp lime juice
- 1/4 tsp salt, or more to taste
- Optional: 1 - 2 jalapenos or other red chilli pepper, minced

** supreme means segmenting and removing the fine skin on the segments. Instructions to supreme are found in several places in this book already. Grapefruit is already known for its bitterness, so to supreme it means that you reduce that taste element.

Once you take the segments from your fruit, squeeze the remaining juice into a bowl. In that bowl whisk all the oil, agave, garlic, lime, salt and chilli. Add the dressing to your onion, grapefruit, avocado and cilantro. Test and adjust agave, salt or lime if necessary.

~ • ~

59. Bruschetta Salsa

The classic Italian snack: A fragrant juxtaposition of basil and tomatoes with olive oil and a strong garlic accent. Characteristically served on toasted Italian style bread or baguette you could also just eat this toast topper as a fabulous salsa. Or top some slices of vegetables or raw breads.

I like to deseed my tomatoes because the mixture is far less sloppy and stays together better. You can choose to keep the seeds if you wish.

Tomato mixture:

- 4 large firm ripe tomatoes, seeded and diced
- 2 tbsp garlic, crushed
- 1/4 cup fresh basil leaves, chopped
- 2 tbsp fresh parsley, chopped
- 2 tsp fresh lemon juice
- 1 tbsp olive oil
- Sea salt and freshly ground black pepper to taste

Choose a base:

- Bread (baguette, sourdough, anything) vegetables or other base and cut into thin slices.
- Rub bread (or other) with garlic
- Add tomato mixture to each piece of bread

~ • ~

60. Fresh Salsa

- 5 ripe medium tomatoes diced (keep or remove seeds)
- 1 small white or red onion finely chopped
- 1/2 cup fresh cilantro/coriander leaves and stalks, chopped
- 1 ear corn, shucked
- 1 cup red capsicum (bell pepper) diced small
- 1/2 cup celery, finely sliced or diced
- 2-3 cloves garlic, minced
- 1 tsp sugar (rapadura or coconut sugar is good, unprocessed and natural)
- 1.5 tbsp fresh lime juice
- Sea salt and pepper to taste
- If you like it spicy add 1 jalapeno finely chopped (or other hot pepper)

Combine all ingredients in a bowl.

Serve as a salad, or with bread or corn fritters or other dish inspired by the flavors.

Options and variations

- I am happy popping in 1/4 tsp of chipotle powder, or some cayenne.
- You can use lemon juice or even apple cider vinegar instead of lime.

~ • ~

61. Ginger Chipotle Salsa

- 3 tomatoes diced
- 2 tsp (or more to taste) chipotle chilli in adobo sauce
- 3 tsp minced ginger
- 1 clove garlic, minced
- 1 green onion sliced finely
- 1 tbsp lime juice
- 1/2 tsp sea salt
- 1/2 tsp sugar (coconut palm, rapadura)

Pulse half of the tomatoes with the rest of the ingredients. Then fold through the other half of the toms to create a chunky salsa. Adjust the heat, salt and lime amounts if necessary and add freshly ground pepper to taste.

~ • ~

62. Limey Tomango Salsa

- 4 medium tomatoes, seeded, chopped small
- 1 mango, flesh chopped small
- 1 small (or 1/2 medium) red onion chopped small
- 3-4 tsp lime juice
- 1/4 cup cilantro (coriander leaves) chopped finely
- 1 tsp cumin
- 1/4 + tsp sea salt (add more to taste)
- Optional: Cracked pepper

Combine the ingredients. As with the "Ginger Chipotle Salsa" you may choose to pulse 2 of your tomatoes and then folding through the rest of the ingredients, to create a more cohesive style salsa.

~ • ~

63. Coconut Papaya Salsa (or Mango)

You could use mango in this salsa or a mango-papaya combination. The best coconut to use would be flaked coconut so you can really feel this under the tooth. If you don't have that then this salsa is equally delicious with shredded coconut.

I have made the ginger optional but I think it really does belong in there. But that's just me! So, combine the following ingredients:

- 2 cups papaya, chopped
- 1 tsp sugar
- 3 tbsp dried coconut flakes (or shreds)
- 3 tbsp lime juice
- 1 chilli pepper (or more to taste)
- 1/4 cup red bell pepper, diced
- 1/4 cup red onion, diced
- 3 tbsp chopped cilantro
- 1 tsp Bragg Liquid Aminos
- Optional (and highly recommended): 1 tsp minced ginger

Options and variations

- Use basil instead of cilantro.
- Use tamari or omit Bragg all together

~ • ~

64. Tomato Mint Salsa

- 4 tomatoes, halved, deseeded then chopped
- 1/2 small red onion, diced
- 1/4 cup mint, chopped finely
- 1 small chilli pepper of your choice, minced
- Zest of 1 medium orange (see next ingredient)
- 1 medium orange, supreme cut, chopped
- 1 tbsp olive oil (or other oil)
- 1 tsp sugar (coconut palm, rapadura or other)
- 1/2 tsp sea salt
- Cracked fresh pepper to taste

Combine your ingredients! Serve and enjoy your salsa.

To supreme your orange, cut the peel off and then remove the segments from the pith with a knife. This will make the orange more tasty.

~ • ~

Dressings, Vinaigrettes, Sauces, Dips, Hummus, Dollop Creams

~ • ~

~ • ~

Dressings, vinaigrettes, sauces, dips, hummus and dollop creams

Learning to create amazing dressings, vinaigrettes, dips and sauces will tantalize your taste buds. You will look forward to your salads and vegetables. And when you know that what you're making is incredibly scrumptious AND healthy, providing you with valuable nutrients you'll feel better about yourself too!

Making good eating choices that are delicious is easier than you thought!

You'll find dressings of various thicknesses and consistencies. Some of the dressing recipes are sweet, some vinegary, others fruity and others tangy. Some are smooth and others are textured.

Taste-testing and taking taste dilution into account

Dressings, by design, have a distinctive or strong taste. They combine a varied mixture of sour (acidic/vinegary), spicy, sweet, sour and salty elements. How you perceive these stronger flavors is determined by your own personal preferences, how you think your 'diners' will receive your cooking and how the dressing combines with the dish you are embellishing.

Remember that the taste of all your dressings will dilute when you add it to salads. If you've never made your own homemade dressings before then you may possibly think that several of my recipes are strong in flavor. This is by design. Dressings have to make some kind of statement. You want to taste them. Of course, most people don't drink a dressing straight. Dressing flavors dilute when placed on a salad. You will have to get used to calibrating your response to take this dilution into account.

Taste-test to take produce variations into account

When you make dressings you will taste test them. This is because produce varies. From batch to batch and piece to piece lemons are more or less sour; chilli peppers are more or less hot; sweeteners appear to have different strengths.

With any recipe with hot chilli peppers, you may want to put in half the amount. Mix. Taste. See if you like it the way it is. Adjust.

Chances are with many dressings from time to time, you will want to adjust salt levels, pepper, lemon, miso, oil, vinegar, garlic, chilli or honey or agave. This is totally normal.

The art of taste-testing

Creating balance in your dressings may take a little practice. So be patient and enjoy the discovery process.

A skilled cook can test a dressing by tasting it from the jar. A newbie to dressing creation may need a little practice to get used to taking dilution into account. Check whether it tastes good on the salad. If you want to, try first to add a teaspoon of dressing to some of your salad ingredients. You may just find that it is perfectly balanced and all you needed to do was balance it with the salad.

However, be brave. For the most part, if this is a first time foray into making your own dressings, make your minor adjustment if you think it needs it, and then calibrate the appeal of the final dish. It is very common for people to make their dressings too mild because they realize afterward they can hardly taste anything in the final dish.

Too much vinegar?

If something is too vinegary (too acidic or too citrus) you can often rebalance the dressing by adding a touch of sweetness. Add a small amount of rapadura or coconut palm sugar, honey or agave.

If you overdo the vinegar to oil ratio then you can add a little more oil. This works particularly well if you're using a good quality aromatic oil.

Too salty?

Too salty and you may need to add more of a base ingredient such as an oil, avocado, silken tofu, more tomato … something that will dull the salt without compromising the output.

Salt or miso? Your choice

In the following recipes you will find that I recommend using sea salt. Feel free to substitute either a mugi (barley), chickpea or light (shiro) miso for this salt for a flavor variation in the following proportion:

½ teaspoon sea salt = 1 tablespoon miso

Purposeful dressings recipe repetition so you can find what you're after

Oh, I have to tell you. I wanted you to find ALL the dressings and dips in this section. So, wherever I have mentioned a sauce that goes with a particular salad in the "Salads" section, rest assured you should also find it right here in "Dressings". That way you'll have the whole kit and caboodle at your fingertips. You'll find this repetition very handy because you can just run your eye through the dressings pages to find your inspiration quickly and efficiently.

So with all that said … here are some wonderful recipes that you will enjoy the taste, color and textures of.

65a. Easy & Delicious Dressing

Nothing beats this dressing for simplicity. Add more or less of any of these ingredients to taste (because tastes vary between lemons and batches of oil and even types of salt! The strength of your lemon and your olive oil changes with the season and type. For olive oil the time of harvest will change how mild or spicy it is. This is one reason why all dressings need taste testing and may need flavor adjustments.

You could add the ingredients into a sealable jar, combine, serve and then store. Another reason why it's called an easy dressing.

This is simply wonderful on a plain leafy salad. Or add in pieces of tomato, avocado, cucumber and generous amounts of basil. See salad section for others! This one I just eyeball it without measuring, straight into the salad! But try these amounts.

- 1 tbsp lemon juice (add more lemon juice as your taste dictates)
- 3 tbsp olive oil
- 1/2 tsp sea salt

Whisk these ingredients together in a bowl.

Options and variations

- Add a tsp of lemon zest, minced.
- Add plenty of ground pepper

65b. 'Easy & Delicious' with a Punch

- Add a crushed garlic clove
- Add a dash of cayenne pepper

~ • ~

65c. Endless 'Easy & Delicious' Varieties

Be adventurous. If you're using a different oil, make it aromatic to make taste your focus. Reserve your plainer tasting oils for other dressings and dips where you need the oil consistency and perhaps are adding them for their specific nutritional profile.

OK, so how about some other ideas for you:

- Finely chop some green herbs: Cilantro, Mint, Basil
- Cumin powder
- Ginger root, minced or grated
- Try walnut oil instead of olive oil
- Sesame oil
- Flaxseed oil
- Smoked or sweet paprika

You're only limited by your imagination. Go on a whim and remember first and foremost, keep it easy!

~ • ~

66a. Basic Vinaigrette

Follow the recommendations below and feel equally satisfied with the different taste sensations you can create when you substitute other high quality cold pressed oils and vinegars without or 'with the mother'. If you're not used to the taste of flaxseed oil then unless you have an immediate love affair with the flavor, introduce it in smaller amounts.

- 2 part cold pressed olive oil (or 1 part olive and 1 part flaxseed oil)
- 1 part apple cider vinegar (I choose Bragg unfiltered organic - yum)
- 1 clove garlic, crushed
- Sea salt to taste (if it's good quality, unrefined you can be generous)
- Cracked pepper
- Optional: Add some Dijon or grain mustard (for a single salad amount add 1/2 tsp mild mustard)

Dressing recommendations

Add more oil if you find it too tangy! But remember flavors dilute when you add them to the salad! The other 'fix' that's handy to keep in mind: If you like the consistency and you need to tone the acidic/vinegary taste, add a very small amount of agave or honey.

~ • ~

66b. Basil Basic

To the "Basic Vinaigrette" add a handful of basil leaves and blend.

~ • ~

67. Sweet & Sour Sesame Asian Dressing

This recipe made its debut as the dressing for "Sweet and Sour Cucumber Salad". To help you relocate it pronto, here it is along with all the other dressings. All you have to do is decide what size your 'part' will be. Perhaps 1 part= 2 tablespoon. That will make half a cup of finished dressing with imperial tablespoons, and 2/3 cup with metric tablespoons.

Sesame oils are not all the same! The ones you find in most supermarkets are likely to be toasted sesame oil. They have a much stronger sesame flavor. In fact sometimes too much toasted sesame oil can be overpowering. Because of the nutritional profile of sesame oil I use raw, cold pressed sesame oil. The black sesame oil is stronger tasting.

If the oil I have doesn't impart that great sesame flavor to my dressing I will add mostly the raw oil (for the superior nutrition) and add a teaspoon or so of the toasted oil, to bolster the taste.

- 1 part oil of choice, I use sesame oil
- 2 parts apple cider vinegar
- 1 part raw honey (my preference) or other sweetener (agave)
- Sea salt (generous)
- Pepper to taste
- Optional pinch of cayenne pepper (or finely chopped red chilli)

Whisk in a bowl until well combined. What you're after is a slightly sweet yet tangy sauce! It's best to taste test this one as you're preparing it.

Options and variations

- Yes, you guessed. Spice it up with a chilli if you wish.
- Add some zing with ginger

~ • ~

68. Thai Satay Dressing

Satay usually uses peanut butter. Here you're using almond butter. There are many people who either have issues with the allergen aspect of peanuts or do not consider them as healthy as almonds. Almonds have an excellent profile. Did you know they are very high in calcium? See the options for important variants!

- 2 tsp sesame oil
- 1/4 cup almond butter
- 1/4 cup coconut water (or water)
- 1 clove garlic minced
- 1 teaspoon of minced ginger
- 3 tsp agave or honey
- 1 tbsp lime or lemon juice
- 1 tbsp Bragg Liquid Aminos
- Chilli pepper to taste. Use powder or fresh minced chilli. As hot as you like
- Optional: 1 tsp tamarind paste (used in authentic Asian tasting food)

I really like to make my dressings in a smallish jar with a wide mouth, that seals well. Or use a bowl of course. If you make more than you need then you have mixed it in the jar and you can simply close the jar after you've used what you need.

To the jar first add and combine the almond butter and water. The paste can sometimes get very thick. Once you have initially combined the nut or seed butter add everything else. Combine well.

IMPORTANT: Taste test to see if you need to add any more Bragg or citrus <u>before</u> thinning with any water. Satay dressings really need some body.

Options and variations

- Make this very creamy by using coconut cream in place of some or all of the water.

Instead of almond butter you can use:

- Sesame butter (tahini)
- Peanut butter
- Cashew or macadamia butter

69. Mango Avocado Dressing

This is a great all-purpose dressing and can be used on green salads or even poured over fruit salad.

- 1 large mango, flesh
- 2 medium avocados, flesh only (or 1 large)
- 1 clove garlic, minced
- Grate the zest of a lemon, to get ½ - 1 tsp for your dressing ... then
- 1 lemon, juiced
- 1 small jalapeño (or other chilli pepper), seeded (keep seeds to increase heat)
- 2 tbsp honey or agave nectar
- 2 tbsp cold pressed olive oil
- 1 tsp apple cider vinegar

Place all ingredients in a blender and process until smooth. This may be thick. Add water or coconut water to thin until desired consistency is achieved.

~ • ~

70a. That Tahina Dressing

It's oh so useful to mix this one up in a jar. Get yourself a nice clean jar. Or, do what I do. I will often make this dressing when I notice that just the right amount of tahina (tahini) remains at the bottom of my jar. This way I use last ounce in the jar and it's all ready to be stored - IF we have any left over.

You may be curious as to why you should mix this in a jar rather than in a bowl. You will experience something rather amazing. When you add fluid to the tahini, whether it's water or Bragg or lemon juice, it actually gets thicker at first.

You need to add the fluid slowly or it will just flick up at you and you'll end up wearing it. Mixing with a spoon in a jar means the mouth of the jar provides you some protection. You will easily recognize (and look for) the turning point in the way this stuff mixes. Have fun!

- 1/4 cup tahini (tahini)
- 3 tsp fresh lemon juice
- 3 tsp tamari or Bragg Liquid Aminos
- 1 clove garlic
- Start with 1/4 cup water

With the tahini in a jar add the lemon juice and tamari or Bragg. Add the garlic at any stage. Start to stir. Add half the water and then just keep stirring and adding water until you achieve a smooth consistency. It should be thick and flowing.

As usual, it's worth taste testing and adjusting. So add salt and pepper to taste if you wish.

Options and variations

A pinch of cayenne or cumin are excellent additions.

~ • ~

70b. Greenified Tahina Dressing

This tahini-based creation is a variation on "That Tahina Dressing" with some green onion and coriander.

You can prepare this in a blender. In which case it still pays to mince your garlic and chop your greens, because you will only pulse your ingredients before adding in the tahini.

If you intend to hand mix your dressing, chop the garlic, cilantro and onion finely enough for your taste then you can mix it in a jar.

- 4 oz tahini
- 1/3 cup lemon juice
- 1-2 cloves garlic, minced
- 1/4 cup cilantro leaves finely chopped
- 1/2 green onion, finely chopped
- 1/2 tsp sea salt

If you're using a blender than pulse everything except the sesame paste. Then add the tahini as you have the blender on low to make a thick paste. Then serve.

Alternatively, combine everything in a jar and stir with a spoon or fork.

~ • ~

71. Blond Lemon Dressing

I love, love, love this dressing. The whole family does. Some of the flavor of this dressing comes from the blond miso. You will find this in your store labeled as shiro miso and is very light in color and the sweetest of the misos. It still has a pleasing saltiness.

- 1/2 cup cashews (soaked and drained if you have time)
- 1/2 cup pine nuts (soaked for 20 mins, drained, if time permits)
- 1/4 cup water
- 3-4 tsps fresh lemon juice. Start with 3 tbsp and work upwards
- Zest of one lemon
- 2 tsps shiro miso

Blend everything together until smooth.

Options and variations

Although it wouldn't stay 'blond', try a variation of this lemony creation with 2 tablespoons of basil leaves, blended.

72. Tomango Dressing

- 1 medium mango, flesh only
- I medium tomato
- 1 tbsp apple cider vinegar or coconut aminos or lemon or lime juice
- Add 1/2 tsp lemon zest
- Add some zing with some grated ginger
- Sea salt and pepper to taste

Place all ingredients in a blender and process until smooth. Add more water to thin until desired consistency is achieved. This is another all-purpose dressing for just about any savory or fruit salad.

73. Sweet Ginger Sauce

- 1/4 cup light flavored oil such as a nut oil or light olive
- 1/2 tsp sea salt or 1 tbsp mugi or chickpea miso
- 4 dates, pit them and soak them in a little water for 15 minutes
- 2 tbsp fresh lemon juice
- 1 clove garlic, minced
- 1 inch or 2.5 cm ginger, minced
- Extra water (if you run out of soak water and need to adjust consistency)

Place all ingredients in a blender (using some soak water from the fruit) and blend until smooth. To adjust consistency add soak water and extra water 1 tablespoon at a time.

Options and variations

- Add finely chopped red chilli for some heat.
- Use equivalent volume dried peaches or apricots instead of dates.

~ • ~

74. Nuts About This Dressing

If you don't have almond butter you can use 2/3 cup of almonds. While the result is not identical it will still work! Soak the almonds first (for 2-8 hours, even overnight) to facilitate a smoother blend. Then drain and rinse them well.

- 3 tbsp almond butter
- 1 garlic clove
- 2 tbsp lemon juice
- 1 tbsp olive oil or other
- 2 dates, pitted and soaked for 20 minutes, keep the soak water
- Sea salt and ground pepper to taste

Place all ingredients in a blender including the date soak water. Blend until smooth. Use the soak water first to create the dressing texture you're after. You can add extra water after the initial blend.

75. Coriander Chipotle Dressing

I like this dressing on a salad with avocado, corn, tomatoes and leaves. Honestly, you could adapt your favorite salad to create a salsa using some of this dressing!

- 1/2 cup pine nuts (soaked 1-2 hours)
- 1/2 cup red bell pepper, deseeded
- 1/3 cup cilantro leaves
- 1 tomato
- 2 tbsp olive oil
- 1-2 tbsp lemon juice
- 1/2 tsp or more chipotle in adobo (or dried chipotle, soaked) to taste
- 2 tbsp coconut water (or water)
- 1 tsp coconut palm sugar, rapadura or liquid sweetener
- 1/2 tsp sea salt and ground pepper to taste

Blend until smooth. You can add extra water to get your desired consistency after the initial blend. Adjust the sweet/salt/citrus/chilli balance if necessary!

76a. Lemon Cashew Dressing 1

The optional addition of caraway seeds is a delightful combination with the lemon.

- 1/2 cup cashews, soaked (about one hour) and drained
- 1 garlic clove
- 2 tbsp lemon juice
- 2 tbsp olive oil or other
- 1 date, pitted and soaked for 20 minutes, keep the soak water
- Sea salt
- Cracked pepper if you wish, to taste

Options and variations

- Add 1 tsp of caraway seeds

Blend all ingredients except for optional caraway seeds, for 20 seconds. Add seeds & pulse through without pulverizing them.

~ • ~

76b. Lemon Cashew Dressing 2

This one has slightly more complex flavor notes. It's yummy.

- 1/2 cup cashews, soaked an hour, rinsed and drained
- 1/2 cup tahini
- 1 garlic clove
- 4 tbsp nutritional yeast flakes
- 2-3 tbsp lemon juice (start with 2)
- 2 tbsp olive oil or other
- 1/2 tsp sea salt
- 3/4 tsp cumin powder (or mild curry)
- 1/2 cup water

Blend until smooth and creamy. Adjust your seasonings and lemon levels. Serve!

~ • ~

77. Sweet Mustard Sauce

A great all-rounder with perfectly balanced flavors.

- 1/4 cup olive oil
- 1 tbsp agave nectar
- 1 clove garlic
- 2-3 tsp dry mustard or 1.5 tsp Dijon or mild mustard (even grain mustard)
- 1/2 tsp ground flaxseed
- 1/2 tsp sea salt
- 2-3 tbsp lemon juice
- 2 tbsp nutritional yeast flakes

Blend until smooth, add water if necessary. Adjust your lemon and mustard flavors to achieve the desired balance.

~ • ~

78. Mustard-Almond Aioli

Aioli is the French name for garlic mayonnaise. This one is a twist on an old classic and surprisingly like a real mayonnaise.

- 3 tbsp apple cider vinegar
- 1/2 lemon, juiced
- 2/3 cup olive oil
- 3 cloves garlic
- 1/3 cup almonds (soaked for 2-8 hours, rinsed and drained if you have time)
- 1 tsp mild mustard (or some mustard powder)
- 1/4 tsp sea salt (and more to taste if necessary)
- 1/4 tsp black pepper, freshly ground
- 1/4 cup of water and more if needed, 1 tbsp at a time.

Blend at a high setting for about 60 seconds until you get a creamy mayonnaise-like dressing. Taste test and check for thickness. This should have the consistency of a 'real' mayonnaise. If the nuts are unsoaked you will need to add more water. Start with a quarter cup and then add a tablespoon or 2 at a time as required.

Even though the dilution on your salad will have an effect, if you feel that there is too much vinegar then add a little oil and or water. The garlic flavor will still shine through.

~ • ~

79. Moroccan Dressing

Spirit yourself away with this North African inspired dressing. It goes well served with a tagine, with a chickpea salad or just a green leafy one. You can spice this one up even more with cayenne, hot paprika or a chilli pepper.

- 1 tsp cumin powder
- 1/2 tsp coriander powder
- 1 tsp smoked paprika or the paprika of your choice
- Juice of 2 lemons (I add about 1/4 cup)
- 3 tsp balsamic vinegar
- 1 tsp ginger, minced
- 1-2 cloves garlic, minced
- 1/4 cup fresh cilantro, chopped
- 1/4 cup olive oil or a good quality nut oil
- 3 tbsp water
- 1 tsp sea salt
- Fresh pepper, 1/4 - 1/2 tsp

When you add your lemon juice start with half the amount. Combine the rest of your ingredients by whisking them together. Taste test and then add the rest of the lemon juice to taste. Definitely a dressing that is better on the salad. My preference is using it on chickpea salads that also have some green leaves.

80. Lemon Ginger Sesame Sauce

- 1-2 cloves garlic, minced
- 1 tsp ginger, minced
- Pinch cayenne pepper
- 1/4 cup oil (mild tasting, with 1 tbsp of the amount as toasted sesame oil)
- 1 tsp lemon zest if you have it
- 3-4 tbsp lemon juice

Whisk all the ingredients together.

Salad recommendations

Add to your salad ... perhaps "Seaweed Salad", "Bountiful Seaweed Salad" or any other salad to which you would like to add a Asian style vinaigrette .

81. Raspberry Vinaigrette

A very fruity, colorful dressing. It's pretty much just fresh raspberries added to a traditional style vinaigrette.

- 1/4 cup raspberries
- 3+ tbsp orange juice
- 2 tbsp olive oil
- 1/2 tbsp lemon juice
- Sea salt and pepper to taste

Blend all ingredients in a blender until smooth. Check the flavor and adjust. It may need more salt than you initially consider to get the balance right. Variability of produce is always an element here and in many dressings so be willing to adjust to create balance of the sweet, salt, and sour.

You may choose to pass the vinaigrette through a sieve to remove any seeds.

~ • ~

82. Balsamic Vinaigrette

- 3 tbsp extra virgin olive oil
- 2 tsp Dijon mustard
- 2 tbsp good quality balsamic vinegar
- Up to 1/4 tsp sea salt (taste test as you go!)
- 1/2 tsp freshly ground black pepper

Whisk in a bowl.

Options and variations

If you are a garlic lover, then mince some garlic and add it to the bowl.

~ • ~

83a. Black Olive Dressing

Goes very well on green leafy salads, Greek salads, salads with mango or nectarine, and is delightful with chickpea or white bean salads.

- 1/4 cup black olives, pitted
- Zest of 1 lemon
- 1/4 cup lemon juice
- 1 tsp fresh oregano or 1/2 tsp dried oregano
- 1 garlic clove
- 1 tsp Dijon mustard
- 1 tsp nutritional yeast or yeast flakes
- 1/4 tsp sea salt
- 1/4 tsp ground pepper
- 1/4 cup olive oil

Blend all ingredients together for 20-30 seconds. To emulsify dressings well, you can add everything except the oil. Blend and then slowly add the oil while the blender is running on a fairly low setting.

~ • ~

83b. Rich Tomato Dressing

Essentially swap out the olives and pop in the tomatoes for this very worthy variation on the "Black Olive Dressing". It will also go very well on green leafy salads, Greek salads, salads with mango or nectarine, and is delightful with chickpea or white bean salads. ;)

- 1/4 cup "Homemade Semi-Dried Tomatoes" (see recipe or use store bought)
- Zest of 1 lemon
- 1/4 cup lemon juice
- 1 tsp fresh oregano or 1/2 tsp dried oregano
- 1 garlic clove
- 1 tsp Dijon mustard
- 1 tsp nutritional yeast or yeast flakes
- 1/4 tsp sea salt
- 1/4 tsp ground pepper
- 1/4 cup olive oil

Blend all ingredients together for 20-30 seconds.

~ • ~

84. Minted Pear Silk

My husband, mother and daughter think this one is divine. Come to think of it, so do I. The clean tastes of mint and pear with the smoothness of cashews will delight you and lift a leafy salad to new heights. Surprisingly subtle, delicious, sublime. It scores 10/10.

- 1/2 cup cashews (soaked if you have time, and drained)
- 1 large ripe pear (or 2 small), remove stork
- 1/2 cup pine nuts (soaked for 20 mins if time permits, drained)
- 1/4 cup water
- 3 tbsp walnut or olive oil
- 1/4 tsp sea salt
- 2-3 tsp apple cider vinegar (start with 2)
- 2 tbsp chopped mint
- 1 tsp shiro miso

Blend until smooth. Add more water or salt or vinegar … if required.

~ • ~

85. Sweet & Spicy Tomato Pasta Sauce

Use this as a sauce for pasta or as a dressing for any salad. A characteristically flavorsome dressing like this complements a simple dish. I have added this one to many a "Super Salad". Instructions for that are found in the chapter on "Salads".

- 1 cup "Homemade Semi-Dried Tomatoes" (or 2/3 cup store-bought dried toms) soaked one hour, keep the water
- 2 soft dates, pitted
- 2 cloves garlic, chopped
- 2 big or 3 medium tomatoes
- 1 tsp dried oregano
- 1/4 cup fresh basil, shredded
- 4 tbsp cold pressed olive oil
- 2 tbsp fresh lemon juice
- A pinch of cayenne or 1 teaspoon sweet paprika

Blend all ingredients in a machine to get desired consistency. Make your adjustments including adding the soak water as you need it.

~ • ~

86. Sesame Vinaigrette Dressing

- 2 1/2 tbsp cold pressed olive oil
- 1 tsp raw sesame tahini
- 1 tbsp lemon juice
- 2 tsp apple cider vinegar (Bragg makes a good one)
- 1 garlic clove, minced
- Sea salt, to taste

You may need to add a few drops of water to thin it down a little. Tahina (or tahini) often thickens the mix into a paste.

~ • ~

87. Mangorient dressing

- 1/2 cup walnuts (you can soak these if you have the time, drain)
- 1/2 cup mango flesh
- 1 lemon, juiced
- 1 tsp cumin powder (or more to taste)
- 1 clove garlic
- 1/2 cup water
- 1/2 cup coriander
- Sea salt, start with 1/4 tsp and add if you desire
- Pepper to taste
- Optional: 1/2 tsp dulse

Blend well. Taste and see if you need either a dash of Bragg Liquid Aminos or a little extra lemon juice. Serve over salad.

If the nuts are unsoaked you will need to add more water. Add a tablespoon or 2 at a time as required.

About sea vegetables and iodine

Sea vegetables are excellent mineral sources. In fact if you're using sea salt and not the iodized table salt variety, then make sure you involve foods that top up your iodine levels. Look later at the recipe for "Mineral Sesame Sprinkles" also known as "Gomasio" which is a wonderful all-purpose dressing (sprinkle) which you can buy or better still, make yourself.

~ • ~

88. Lemon-Ginger Vinaigrette

Lemon and ginger has got to be one of my favorite combinations. I drink gallons of lemon and ginger tea every week. For years now. So enjoy this vinaigrette with a fresh tang of lemon and the pleasing bite of ginger.

- 3 tbsp olive oil
- 1 tbsp lemon juice
- 1/2 cup balsamic vinegar
- 1 tsp ginger, minced (start with 1/2 tsp and add to taste)
- 1 clove garlic, minced
- Sea salt and pepper to taste

Whisk all ingredients in a bowl.

Options and variations

Use different types of oils. Sesame oil, or walnut, macadamia or hazelnut oil.

~ • ~

89. Smooth Green Caesar Dressing

This light yet creamy dressing is healthy, delicious and reminds me of Caesar dressings. The strength of your tahini paste can vary from mild to quite strong and earthy. So as much as I would love to give you THE amount to add, I do have to figure in possible variations that could occur in your kitchen. So start with less. Taste the dressing and see if you like it with the small amount. Too much tahini can be harder to adjust for than just about any other ingredient!

- 3 tbsp lemon juice, fresh (start with 2 and add to taste)
- 2 tbsp tahini (metric start with 1.5)
- 1/2 avocado
- 1 clove garlic
- 1 tsp ginger, grated
- 1/4 tsp sea salt
- A good amount of fresh cracked pepper, at least 1/4 tsp
- 1/2 cup water
- Optional: 1/4 tsp dulse (it's better with dulse)
- Optional 1-2 tsp capers

If you don't have a blender, mash the avocado with a fork and combine everything together by hand. It's obviously creamier when you use a blender. Test the taste after combining. You may like to add some more lemon juice, some salt, or tahini 1 teaspoon at a time.

Options and variations

If you don't have any avocado, then you can always substitute either silken tofu or some oil. Add in 2 tablespoons of olive oil (and then add one teaspoon at a time). Imperial and metric tablespoons are different so this will take those differences into account!

~ • ~

90. Classic Caesar Dressing

This is another Caesar Dressing with that salty hint of capers. The recipe is for either oil-free (using silken tofu) or by using a complementary oil. You actually could use 1/2 cup of soaked cashews or pine nuts.

- 1/4 cup lemon juice
- 1 clove garlic
- 2 tsp mustard (Dijon or grain, I like the Maille brand)
- 2-3 tsp capers (start with 2 and then taste test)
- 1 tsp nutritional yeast or 1.5 tsp yeast flakes
- 1/4 tsp ground fresh pepper
- 1/4 tsp sea salt
- Optional 1/4 tsp dulse
- **1/2 cup soft tofu
- OR: ½ cup light tasting oil, such as sunflower oil, light olive oil (or a late harvest olive oil with milder flavor).

Garnish

Some fresh herbs perhaps?

Options and variations

If you're using the tofu then put everything in the blender. If using oil then add all but the oil and blend, Then add the oil a little at a time. This helps to emulsify and incorporate the ingredients well. Good old whisking works well too!

**Remember, you have the choice to use EITHER soft tofu OR soaked cashews or pine nuts OR oil.

This tasty sauce will last for up to a week in the fridge.

~ • ~

91. Robert's Favorite Dressing

We sometimes prepare a jar of this lovely red dressing at home and then use it on various salads throughout the week.

While this dressing is great with olive oil I also really like it with a good quality walnut or hazelnut oil.

You will zip this one in a blender to make it good and smooth. I really like the fresh, sweet, and spicy notes. Don't have a chilli? Add a good pinch of cayenne. Want to avoid the oil? Make up for it with silken tofu. While Robert and I really like this spicy, our daughter gives it 9 out of 10 when it is chilli-free! We even add this to stir fries.

To a blender add

- Flesh of 1 red pepper (capsicum), no seeds
- 2 tbsp lime juice
- 3 tsp apple cider vinegar
- 1/4 cup oil and 1/4 cup silken tofu (see options below))
- **3 dried apricots (soaked to soften)
- 1 small clove garlic chopped
- 1 tsp cumin
- 1/4 tsp salt
- A couple of grinds of fresh black pepper
- 1 small chilli (you choose the heat level). Remove seeds, chop and if unsure, add a portion at a time

Options and variations

- Instead of oil and silken tofu you can use 1/2 cup of a light tasting (olive or nut) oil
- **Substitute 2 soaked dried peach halves or 1/4 cup dried raisins (sultanas)

Blend and serve!

Salad recommendations

This dressing works well with any simple green leafy salad. Or pair it with a more complex "Super Salad" , "Avocado Grapefruit Salad" , any "Slaw" or even "Greek Salad".

~ • ~

92. Raw Mayonnaise

This is so good that my hubby who LOVES mayonnaise started using this instead of the regular stuff, from the day I starting making this.

- 1 cup raw cashews (if time, soaked, rinsed, drained)
- 1/2 tsp sweet paprika
- 2 cloves garlic
- 1 tsp onion powder (gives a good flavor but not necessary if you don't have it)
- 3 tbsp lemon juice (start with 2)
- 3 tbsp olive oil or other (avocado oil or sunflower, or raw sesame oil)
- 2 tbsp water
- 1/4 tsp sea salt (plus more to taste)
- 1/4 pepper to taste

Add all ingredients but hold back on the lemon to start with, especially if you are using metric spoons. In my kitchen with metric I used 2 tablespoons plus 1 teaspoon of lemon juice. That actually equates to 3 tablespoons (in the US). This is why I recommend that to play it safe you start with 2 tablespoons of lemon and add in to taste.

Blend until smooth. Adjust with lemon juice, salt and pepper. Add water only if needed to thin. If the nuts are unsoaked you will need to add more water. Start with a quarter cup and then add a tablespoon or 2 at a time as required.

Options and variations

- I routinely use 1/4 teaspoon smoked paprika instead of the sweet one.
- Add in 2 tbsp parsley chopped for a Herbed Mayonnaise. Pulse it through.

If your blender needs more bulk than is provided for in the recipe

This seems odd, but if you have a larger capacity blender some recipes may not have the bulk of ingredients that will create a smooth blend of all the ingredients. In my new blender this occurs with my "Raw Mayonnaise" and "Mustard-Almond Aioli" recipes.

In both cases I have often had to add a tablespoon at a time of each oil and water to bulk up the ingredients so that the blades can completely pulverize everything.

~ • ~

93. Cut Me Some Flax Dressing

Flaxseed oil (and the seeds, naturally) have high levels of omega 3 fatty acids. You can use flaxseed oil in place of any suggested oil in this book. It is said to have high anti-inflammatory benefits. So use it anywhere, not just in this vinaigrette.

Just a cautionary word: In order to use it liberally on anything, you may need to get used to the taste of flaxseed oil. But when you do, you may very well just love it. For example, on the very odd occasion that I eat a slice of toast, I may use flax oil and sprinkle generously with ground sea salt!

- 2 tbsp flaxseed oil
- 5-6 tsp lemon juice (start with 4 and work up)
- 1 clove garlic, minced
- 2 tsp dulse flakes
- 1 sprinkle of cayenne
- 1/4 tsp sea salt
- 1/2 scant tsp light miso

Blend (or whisk) serve, store!

Options and variations

After having lavishly praised the humble flax, it behoves you to know that if you want to substitute walnut oil or hazelnut oil to create different flavors then go right ahead!

~ • ~

94. Orange Ginger Vinaigrette

Ginger is such a great flavor with citrus. You could blend this dressing. But equally you can whisk it. If you do choose to whisk, then you need your ginger to be well incorporated.

My best ginger recommendation is to always keep some in the fridge AND always keep some in the freezer. If you want to feel the ginger 'under the tooth' use the fresh stuff.

If you want it to be distributed right through just as it would be if you were using ginger powder, then grate your frozen ginger with a zester or fine grater. It's great! Or is that, it's grate? Ummm, sorry.

The use of smoked paprika makes this very delectable.

- 1/2 cup fresh squeezed orange juice
- 2 tbsp vinegar (your choice, vary the taste)
- 2 tbsp olive oil
- 1/2 tsp sea salt
- 1/4 tsp or more of fresh pepper
- 1 tsp ginger, minced (see note above about using frozen ginger)
- 1/4 tsp smoked paprika (or paprika of your choice, or pinch of cayenne)

Whisk together and then add to your salad

Options and variations

- Add 1 tbsp fresh mint, minced
- Add 1 tbsp fresh tarragon, minced
- Add some minced garlic
- Instead of smoked paprika you could also try some chipotle chilli powder

~ • ~

95. Fragrant Tomato Vinaigrette

Enjoy this beautiful red dressing with the strong accent of tomato that can only come from dried morsels. Remember there is a super simple recipe for "Homemade Semi-dried Tomatoes" near the back of this book in the "Garnishes and Snacks" chapter.

As with any vinaigrette part of the burst of flavor is due to the vinegar and other acid ingredients. Hence the name! So with this recipe you have 3 combined teaspoons of vinegar and lemon juice. Substitute in other vinegars if you wish.

- 2 tbsp chopped "Homemade Semi-dried Tomatoes" (see recipe) or use store-bought dried tomatoes
- 1 tbsp sesame seeds
- 1 tsp tahini
- 3 tbsp olive oil
- 1/4 tsp cumin
- 2 tsp lemon juice, fresh is best
- 1 tsp apple cider vinegar
- 1 clove garlic
- Up to 1/4 tsp sea salt

Blend until smooth.

You can actually whisk these ingredients together too. If you want to do that then you will have to mince the tomatoes very well as well as mince the garlic.

Taste test and adjust your dressing to your taste with salt, lemon or oil.

Remember that if you find your dressing unbalanced or too vinegary, try adding a spoonful of sugar (coconut palm or rapadura are my crystalline sugars of choice) or a little liquid sweetener.

~ • ~

96. White Wine Dressing

The recipe below makes 2/3 of a cup of dressing. Note that using a good quality white wine is going to make a big difference to the product!

- 2-3 tbsp white wine (make it a good one!) 2 metric (Europe and Australia), 3 imperial (in the US).
- 1/4 cup lemon juice
- 1 tsp honey
- 1/3 cup extra virgin olive oil
- Sea salt and pepper to taste

Whisk the first 3 ingredients (everything but the oil). Keep whisking as you gradually add the oil in to form an emulsified dressing. Taste test. Adjust your dressing with more wine (!) salt, pepper, or ...

Options and variations

- Consider portioning out half of your dressing and adding a tbsp or so of finely chopped (minced) chives, basil, mint or parsley. You'll have 2 dressings for the price of 1.
- 1/2 teaspoon or more of lemon (or orange) zest is a lovely touch.
- Test this with some red wine instead!

~ • ~

97. Chipotle and Orange Dressing

Mmmmm. I hope you enjoy this one even half as much as I do. Adjust the heat level on this dressing as desired by adding more (or less) chipotle. You know, Robert and I really love chipotle, so we always have some chipotle powder on hand when we don't want to use the tinned variety. It's great sprinkled on, well, just about anything! So if you don't have the tinned fruit, then use the powder.

- 2 tsp orange zest
- 1/3 cup fresh orange juice
- 2/3 cup silken tofu
- 1 tbsp shiro or light miso
- 2 tbsp balsamic vinegar
- 1/2 tsp chipotle (use tinned chipotle in adobo or soak a chilli)
- 2 tbsp honey
- 1/4 cup water
- Sea salt to taste (I use about 1/4 tsp)
- Fresh cracked pepper to taste

Options and variations

If you would like to make your dressing thicker then here are 3 ideas:

- Add another 1/3 cup tofu
- Or add some olive or other oil
- Or use 1/2 cup of soaked cashews

For a delicious variation that creates a new dressing

Add 4 teaspoons tahini (sesame paste). This thickens the dressing and also produces a simply delicious new sauce.

~ • ~

98. Siam Sesame Dressing

This is definitely one of my favorite dressings. You will notice that I have said to include a teaspoon of Bragg Liquid Aminos if you have it. In my opinion, if you like Asian flavors then the Bragg Amino dressing is a wonderful substitute for the fish sauce that you find in many dishes in South East Asia.

The more you blend this one, the smoother it becomes.

- 1/4 cup lime juice
- 1/4 cup basil, chopped
- 1/4 cup cilantro, chopped
- 1/4 cup mint, chopped
- 4 tsp shiro or light miso
- 1 clove garlic
- 1 tsp ginger, minced
- 4 tsp honey
- 1/4 cup sesame seeds
- 1 tsp sesame oil
- 1 tsp Bragg Liquid Aminos (if you have it, if not, omit)
- 2/3 cup water
- Zest of 1 lime
- 1 small seeded chilli (as always, chilli is added 'to taste')

Blend 'er up and serve.

Salad recommendations

Just superb with "Kelp Noodle Salads" and any salad where you wish to be transported to Asia in a culinary way! Almost any selection of salad ingredients will enjoy the Siamese touch. For example the seemingly unlikely candidates, "Simply Zucchini" or "Chickpea Salad" would be worthy of experimentation with this decidedly green sauce!

99. Honey Spice Vinaigrette

- 1/4 cup olive, walnut or hazelnut oil
- 1 tbsp red wine vinegar
- 1/4 tsp sea salt
- A good grinding of fresh pepper
- 1/4 tsp cinnamon
- 1/4 tsp cumin
- 1 tsp honey

Whisk all the dressing ingredients except the oil. Then add the oil to emulsify the dressing. Adjust your dressing (with honey, salt, spice or vinegar). Combine with the salad ingredients and serve.

100a. Mang-nificence Dressing

As the name implies, it's magnificent. Sweet, spicy, scrumptious. Robert and I both gives this a 10. I actually make double the amount because I really love it.

- 2 tbsp fresh orange juice
- 2 tbsp fresh lime juice
- 1/2 cup mango flesh
- 2 tbsp cold-pressed oil of your choice
- 1 clove garlic, minced
- Add fresh deseeded chilli, minced, to taste
- Sea salt and pepper to taste

Blend!

Salad recommendations

I like this on fruit salads, leafy salads, chickpea salads. Any salads! I like it by the spoonful.

100b. Cumin-Scented Mang-nificence

The same dressing with cumin powder in it.

- Add 1/2 tsp cumin.

~ • ~

101. Dijon & Tarragon Dressing

- 2 tbsp fresh tarragon leaves , chopped small (or 2 tsp dried herb)
- 1 clove garlic, minced
- 1/3 cup oil (olive or walnut or hazelnut work well)
- 2 tsp Dijon mustard
- 1/4 tsp sea salt
- 1/4 tsp pepper
- 1 tsp nutritional yeast or yeast flakes
- Zest of a lemon (about a tsp)
- 1-2 tbsp lemon juice

Because this dressing has the sour or acid taste of the mustard, take it easy when adding the lemon juice so you keep the flavors well balanced. Add 1 tablespoon first and then when you're close to the desired outcome, add 1 teaspoon at a time.

Blend this dressing. If you're just whisking this dressing make sure the garlic and tarragon are finely minced.

~ • ~

102. Spiced Apricot Vinaigrette

Guess what? This is my 10 year old's favorite vinaigrette. I couldn't believe it when she told me. A sweet concoction with a hint of curry and a good tangy note to balance it. Taste testing and adjusting is a skill you will learn to master when you create more and more delicious dressings and understand how the flavors mix and complement your salads.

The softer your dried apricots become the smoother and rounder the taste and the easier to blend them. So soak them until soft. I actually use organic non-sulfured dried apricots. These are not bright orange (that's what the sulfur does). They are dark orange and brown. The sweetness is sensational. A natural, deep, sweet flavor that you cannot get with the bright orange ones. So see if you can get them. I give them to our girl. They're her kind of candy.

- 3 dried apricots, chopped, soaked 30 mins, reserve the soak water
- 1/2 cup good quality wine, champagne or rice vinegar
- Either 3 tbsp macadamia or hazelnut oil (or oil of choice)
- OR 1/4 cup silken tofu
- 2 tsp curry powder (choose mild or med)
- 1/4 tsp cumin
- 1/4 tsp cardamom
- 1/4 tsp sea salt (or more)
- Fresh ground pepper to taste (generous)

If you need any extra fluid at all, use the soak water.

Blend, test and adjust your spices if necessary. Serve!

Options and variations

- Make this a Spiced Peach Vinaigrette by using 2 dried peach halves soaked.
- Make this a Spiced Date Vinaigrette by using 3 medjool dates, soaked.

~ • ~

103. Creamy Garlicky Sauce

Garlic lovers will adore this. Great as a sauce or dip. Add extra garlic (depending on your taste). You could make this without the capers and dill for another beautiful yet different experience.

- 1 cup pine nuts, soaked for 1-2 hours, drained
- 1 tsp capers
- 1 tsp dill (dried or fresh)
- 1/4 tomato
- 1/2 tsp sea salt
- 1 clove garlic
- 4 tbsp olive oil
- 1 squeeze of lemon juice

Adjust the consistency with extra water if you need to.

Options and variations

- Add extra dill or capers, garlic or salt to change the flavor profile. Yummy.

~ • ~

Kinda Sorta Sour Crème Reprise

Yes I absolutely know I have included this recipe exactly the same elsewhere in this book. I didn't count it twice though! I just wanted to make sure it's where the guacamoles are in the salad section of the book so you can see it when you need it. So there!

In case you didn't see this recipe before here is that true story about my mom again:

My mom was over for lunch and I prepared this mock sour cream. I offered to give her some to take home. She didn't want to take it home because she didn't want any more dairy that day. After I giggled and she found out that there's no dairy in there at all, she took it ALL home!

The recipe will make something semi-fluid. That's perfect for use as a dressing. If you want to use this as a dollop crème, one that you can place on top of a salad, a guacamole or salsa for example then add 1/4 (to 1/3) cup of avocado and then blend again until smooth. This will create a wonderfully thick sour crème that will hold its own. I don't like to add too much avocado otherwise the color changes and it ends up being a guacamole. About 1/4 cup works really well.

- 1/2 tsp sea salt
- 1 clove garlic chopped
- 1 tsp agave syrup or honey
- 3 tbsp lemon juice
- 1/2 cup water
- 1 cup pine nuts (soaked for 1 hour, drained)

Blend it, baby! Make it smooth.

Taste test it. You may choose to add more lemon or salt.

Options and variations

- Remember to add 1/4 cup avocado if you want a dollop consistency.
- Stir through some minced fresh herbs.

~ • ~

104. Creamy Dressing Base

Use this dressing as a base you can play around with by adding other flavors. My family likes basic creamy sauce on its own with zucchini noodles. Spiral grate 2-3 zucchini for a side dish for a family. 5 minutes before you serve your meal add your super simple dressing. Here it is:

Dressing

- 1 small-medium clove garlic
- 1/2 cup water
- 1/2 cup cashews
- 1/2 cup pine nuts
- 1/4 tsp sea salt
- 1/4 tsp pepper (fresh ground is best)

Place your dressing ingredients in the blender and process until smooth.

~ • ~

105. Red Cream Dressing

This dressing is similar to the "Creamy Dressing Base" with some additions to add complexity to the flavor.

- 1 small-medium clove garlic
- 1/2 cup water
- 1/2 cup cashews
- 1/2 cup pine nuts
- 1/4 tsp sea salt
- 1/4 tsp pepper (fresh ground is best)
- 1/2 cup red pepper (capsicum)
- 2 tsp apple cider vinegar
- A squirt of Bragg Liquid Aminos or Coconut Aminos
- 1/4 cup parsley

Place in a blender! Turn the blender on and blend until smooth

Options and variations

- 1/2 tsp smoked or sweet paprika

~ • ~

Hummus Recipes

These days there are all kinds of hummus recipes. I have included several (more than enough) reliable recipes.

Hummus is so versatile. Use it as a thick dip or as a thinner dressing. For dipping, cut up vegetables such as sticks of carrot, celery, red pepper, cucumbers, broccoli and cauliflower florets. Anything you like! You can dip crackers and bread too!

If using it as a dressing then you may like to dilute it a little more with water or even olive oil, and make it a little more lemony!

Garnish

Most dips, creams, guacamoles and salads look even more delectable when garnished. The homogeneous color of the hummus with its texture make a good splash of color very impressive.

Think of garnishing with black pepper, a swish of avocado or olive oil (even dark rich pumpkin seed oil). How about paprika or chipotle or cayenne? Some chopped herbs.

~ • ~

106. Regular Hummus

- 1-2 cloves garlic, minced
- 1 can of garbanzo beans (chickpeas), drained
- 3 tbsp tahini
- 1/2 tsp sea salt
- 1/4 tsp (or more) ground cumin
- 1-3 tbsp fresh lemon juice (add the right amount according to your taste)
- Add water, if necessary

Place all ingredients up to the lemon juice and water. Add 1 tablespoon of the lemon juice. Blend until smooth maybe with a little water. Taste test and add second and third tablespoons of lemon juice and/or additional salt, as desired.

If hummus seems too thick, stir in water 1 tablespoon at a time. Even add a slurp of olive oil.

~ • ~

107. Sprouted hummus

Try the same recipe as "Regular Hummus" above. BUT instead of adding cooked garbanzo beans, you can make a raw chickpea hummus by soaking and then sprouting your beans. Once your beans have sprouted and have little tails of about 1cm or ½ inch you basically follow the recipe above. Here it is for you!

- 1.5 cups garbanzo beans (chickpeas), sprouted
- 1-2 cloves garlic, minced
- 3 tbsp tahini
- 1/2 tsp sea salt
- 1/4 tsp (or more) ground cumin
- 1-3 tbsp fresh lemon juice (add the right amount according to your taste)
- Add water, if necessary

Place everything except the lemon juice and water in the blender. Add just 1 tablespoon of the lemon juice and then blend until smooth. Taste and add second and third tablespoons of lemon juice and/or additional salt, as desired.

If hummus seems too thick, stir in water 1 tablespoon at a time. Even add a slurp of olive oil.

Garnish

Splash on some oil, sprinkle on some herbs, dust with some colorful cayenne or paprika, zaatar or sumac.

~ • ~

108. Raw Nut Hummus using Macadamias and or Cashews

This is definitely my favorite hummus recipe.

There are easier recipes but this one is very nutritious and extremely delicious. By the way US tablespoons are smaller than metric ones and so this is why in other recipes I sometimes recommend teaspoon amounts so those in metric countries don't overdo it!

- 1.5 cups raw macadamia and or cashew nuts, soaked for a few hours
- 4 tbsp lemon juice (60 ml or 3 tbsp metric)
- 3 tbsp olive oil (40 ml or 2 tbsp metric)
- 3 tbsp tahini or sesame paste (40 ml or 2 tbsp metric)
- 1/2 tsp salt OR instead of salt you could add a tbsp of mugi or chickpea miso
- 1 small clove of garlic
- 2/3 cup of filtered water
- A dash of Bragg Liquid Aminos
- Salt and pepper to taste

Start by using only 1/2 cup of water first and reserve the last little bit just in case you need to thin the hummus after you have already blended it. Place the ingredients in a blender, put the lid on(!) and turn the thing on! Blend until smooth.

Options and variations

It's important to taste-test your hummus. If you find it needing more flavor focus, it may simply need a little more Bragg, salt, lemon juice or tahini. You really cannot go wrong.

- A final suggestion is to add yeast flakes, say, 1 tablespoon.

~ • ~

109. Sundried Tomato Hummus

More tomato less hummus in this one! If you wanted to, you can actually use chickpeas (garbanzo beans), chickpea sprouts or cashews. I have suggested macadamias in this recipe.

- 1/3 cup "Homemade Semi-dried Tomatoes" (see recipe) or store-bought dried tomatoes
- 1/2 cup macadamia (see note above)
- 3 tbsp tahini or sesame paste (2 tbsp metric)
- 3 tbsp lemon juice (3 tbsp metric)
- 1/4 tsp natural sea salt
- 1/2 cup water (or more) OR instead add a 1/2 tbsp mugi or genmai miso
- Fresh pepper to taste
- Optional: 1 tbsp olive oil
- Optional: 1 small clove of garlic

Place the ingredients in a blender, put the lid on(!) and turn the thing on! Blend until smooth.

~ • ~

110. Raw Zucchini Hummus

- 1 zucchini, chopped
- Garlic to taste (1-2 small cloves)
- 1/4 cup lemon juice
- 1/2 tsp salt
- 1/2 tsp cumin
- 1/2 cup raw tahini
- 2 tbsp olive oil
- Optional: Add cayenne pepper
- Optionally add a couple of tablespoons of raw sesame seeds

Simply blend this until smooth!

Garnish

Remember that you can garnish with herbs, a splash of oil, some paprika, pepper, sumac, any seeds or decorative and tasty addition.

111. Roasted Red Pepper Hummus

- Flesh of 1 large red pepper, either roasted whole in a hot oven, or simply discard the stalk and seeds, brush the flesh with a touch of olive oil and broil (grill), until the skin blisters and the flesh is soft (turning once)
- Garlic to taste (1-2 medium cloves)
- 3 tsp lemon juice
- 1/2 tsp salt
- 1/4 tsp cumin
- 1 can of garbanzo beans (chickpeas), drained
- 1/2 cup chopped parsley
- 2 tbsp raw tahini
- 1 tbsp olive oil
- Optional: Add cayenne pepper and pepper to taste

Simply blend this until smooth! Add water 1 tablespoon at a time if you need to thin it.

Options and variations

- Consider fresh chilli added into the recipe, and substituting nuts instead of the chickpeas.
- Add your garnishes

~ • ~

112. Beet This Hummus

Raw beet or cooked beet? I leave it entirely up to you!

- 1/2 cup beet, peeled cubed
- Garlic to taste (1-2 medium cloves)
- 1/4 cup lemon juice
- 1/4 tsp salt
- Black pepper to taste
- 1 tbsp nutritional yeast flakes or a squirt of Bragg Liquid Aminos
- 1/4 tsp sumac or coriander
- 1/2 cup tahini
- 1 can garbanzo beans (chickpeas)
- 1 can white beans (cannellini beans)
- 2+ tbsp olive oil

Add all ingredients to the blender except oil and blend. Then add olive oil to the machine as it runs, 1 tablespoon at a time until you get the desired consistency.

Options and variations

For a less raw version you can steam the beet and roast your garlic.

~ • ~

113. Cilantro White Bean Hummus

- 1 can cannellini beans (I choose organic)
- Garlic to taste (1-2 small cloves)
- 2 tbsp cilantro chopped
- 1 tbsp Bragg Liquid Aminos
- 1 pinch sea salt
- 1 tsp cumin
- 1/2 tsp grated ginger
- 1 tbsp tahini and 3 tbsp olive oil (or just 4 tbsp olive oil)
- Optional: Add cayenne pepper
- You may need a few drops of water to thin it especially if you are adding the tahini.

Simply blend this until smooth! Those using metric tablespoons remember to hold back on putting in the entire amount of oil at one time.

Options and variations

If you want to omit the tahini, add in an extra tablespoon of olive oil.

Garnish

Garnish with something colorful.

~ • ~

114. Sunflower Herb Pâté

Once again you can change this recipe using different seeds and nuts and marry them with different herbs.

Use as a dip, or a spread. I like to spread it on nori (seaweed), on lettuce leaves or crispbreads. Take a look in "Garnishes and Snacks" for some ideas. Specifically see the recipe for "Pâtés for Nori or Sushi Rolls".

- 2 cups total sunflower and/or pumpkin seeds (soaked for 2 hours, rinsed, drained)
- 1/2 cup fresh basil leaves
- 1 clove of garlic (optional)
- 1 tbsp raw tahini (optional)
- Juice of 1 lemon
- 1/4 tsp of sea salt
- A pinch or 2 of coriander powder, sweet or smoked paprika, or cumin or cayenne
- 1 tsp apple cider vinegar
- 2 tbsp flaxseed oil or olive oil

Process in your blender. You don't have to make this smooth. If you like to feel some coarser texture, then pulse in your blender. If you are making this recipe to line your nori rolls then having texture is really worthwhile.

Taste test and adjust your seasonings and then pulse again until you get the right consistency.

Options and variations

Instead of basil leaves, try different fresh herbs or dried herbs.

- Try oregano, rosemary, thyme or tarragon

~ • ~

115. Simply Sunflower Pâté

- 2 cups sunflower seeds, soaked 1-2 hours and drained
- 1 cup almonds, soaked up to 8 hours, rinsed, drained
- 1/2 cup water
- 1/4 cup lemon juice
- 1/3 cup celery chopped small
- 1/4 cup minced red onion
- 1/4 cup minced parsley
- 3/4 tsp salt

Blend until smooth or the desired consistency.

~ • ~

116. Sundried Tomato Sunflower Pâté

Another great pâté variation where "Homemade Semi-Dried Tomatoes" or store-bought sun dried tomatoes take the place of almonds.

- 2 cups sunflower seeds, soaked 1-2 hours and drained
- 2/3 cup Homemade Semi-Dried Tomatoes (or a little less sundried toms), chopped
- 1/2 cup water to soak the chopped tomatoes for 30-60 mins)
- 1/4 cup lemon juice
- 1/3 cup celery chopped small
- 1/4 cup minced red onion
- 1/4 cup minced parsley
- 3/4 tsp salt

Blend until smooth or the desired consistency.

~ • ~

117. Sunflower Macadamia Dip

- 1 cup raw macadamia nuts soaked overnight
- 1 cup sunflower seeds soaked for 1-8 hours
- 1 clove garlic chopped
- 1 tbsp lemon juice
- 1.5 tbsp miso (metric, start with 1 tbsp)
- 2 tbsp minced onion
- 1/4 cup water

Blend until smooth.

You may need to add a little more water (teaspoon at a time).

Recommendations

- Use in nori rolls, wrap in lettuce or flatbreads.
- Use as a regular dip for vegetable crudités.

~ • ~

118. Pesto – With or Without Cheese

You'll be surprised how delicious a pesto can be without cheese! In my experience often cheese is added to make up for an unbalanced pesto. So see what you can do to create a great tasting dip or sauce that is not reliant on cheese. Then add it in if you want.

- 1 bunch basil leaves (about 2-3 cups usually)
- 1/2 cup pine nuts
- 1 clove (or more) garlic
- 1/2 tsp salt and more to taste if necessary
- 1/4 cup olive oil
- 2-3 tsp yeast flakes (start with one)
- Optional: Add in some shiro or light miso to taste (1-2 tsp)

I prefer a pesto where the pine nuts are not too finely ground. So I suggest reserving at least half your pine nuts and firstly blending to break your basil leaves down. Then add the rest of your nuts and combine until you have the right consistency.

Place the ingredients in a blender. Blend and add more olive oil until right thickness. Taste test and add more yeast (or add cheese).

Options and variations

- Feel free to add grated parmesan or other similar cheese (to taste: 2 tbsp-1/4 cup)

119. Olive and Tomato Pesto

Use this as a dip for vegetables or a spread on crackers. Thinned down a little it can be easily used as a sauce for pasta. Zucchini noodles anyone? You can buy your tomatoes or use the recipe at the end of this book for "Homemade Semi-Dried Tomatoes".

- 1/2 cup "Homemade Semi-Dried Tomatoes" or sundried tomatoes soaked in just enough water, reserve the soak water if you want to make a sauce
- 2 tbsp of pine nuts
- 1/2 tsp sea salt
- Pepper to taste
- 1 handful of kalamata (or other) olives, pitted
- Fresh herbs to taste, parsley, oregano or basil

Blend the ingredients together until you get desired consistency. Add the soak water for taste and for thinning into a sauce.

120. Pistachio Pesto

Purchase your pistachios unsalted and already out of their shells. Then combine these ingredients:

- 4 tbsp extra virgin olive oil
- 1 cup basil leaves
- 2-3 cloves garlic
- 1 cup pistachios, shelled, unsalted, soaked for 2+ hours, drained
- 1/4 tsp sea salt
- Cracked pepper to taste

If you need a very smooth pesto just throw everything in the blender at once. However if you like a little crunch then try what I sometimes do: I like to reserve half of the pistachios while I blend the rest of the ingredients. When the leaves are well pulverized I then add the other pistachios and pulse and blend until it's the way I like it. That way I can control the texture.

Options and variations

I like the alliteration of Peppered Pistachio Pesto. Luckily I like the taste too. Just add more pepper.

You may need some extra tang with a dash of lemon juice or some yeast flakes.

~ • ~

Hey Pesto: Ten Delicious Pesto Ideas

You can make a pesto out of just about anything. You don't just need pine nuts and basil. Pestos usually have oil, garlic and sea salt. You can use yeast flakes or miso. Lemon juice or some apple cider vinegar.

Experiment with the pesto recipes in this book and then using similar proportions try your own inventions. Here are some suggestions:

Coriander (cilantro leaves and stalks) with walnuts and sea salt and olive oil

Parsley, garlic, salt and olive oil. This is a beautiful French invention called a Persillade (pronounced Pear-see-yahd)

Basil and pistachio

Rocket, walnut, pepper

Macadamia and parsley

Basil and cashew

Or cashew and other herbs

Almonds, sundried tomato and basil

Pumpkin, brazil nuts, lemon juice, and mixed fresh parsley, basil and dill

Your favorite nut with "**Homemade Semi-Dried Tomatoes**"

~ • ~

121. Rawquefort (Blue Uncheese) Dressing

Blue vein cheese has a particular taste that is sharp, salty and pungent all at the same time. Robert and I were once at a winery (which became our favorite winery that day about 20 years ago) where we attended a wine tasting.

At the end of the session we tasted a sweet dessert wine and with it a blue cheese. Well, having neither really liked either, all of a sudden we loved both.

This vegan (yes dairy-free) dressing or dip really has the saltiness and the reminiscences of blue cheese.

What I learned at that (organic) winery 2 decades ago is this: Blue cheese or blue cheese-like flavors go exceedingly well with sweet fruit.

I like to soak the nuts for this dip. But it won't really compromise the flavor if you don't. You may have a less smooth dressing though (if your blender is not up to the task).

Dressing

- 1/2 small onion (or 1 scallion)
- 1 small - medium garlic clove
- 1/4 cup apple cider vinegar (remove 1 tbsp and set aside just in case you think the resultant dressing needs to have it added back in)
- 3 tsp lemon juice, fresh
- 1/2 cup macadamia nuts (soaked, rinsed, drained)
- 1 cup cashews (soaked if possible, drained)
- 1 tsp sea salt
- 1 tsp fresh pepper ground
- 1/4 cup parsley
- 1/4 cup water

Place everything in a blender and blend away!

If the nuts are unsoaked you will need to add more water. Start with a quarter cup and then add a tablespoon or 2 at a time as required.

Recommendation

- Try using rosemary instead of parsley.
- Pair this dressing with a salad that has one or 2 sweet elements in it. Perhaps some mango or some carrot and apple.
- Use this as a dip for crudités.

~ • ~

122. Baba Ghanouj

- 1 eggplant (medium sized)
- 1 tbsp tahini
- 3 cloves garlic
- 1 tbsp minced onion (optional)
- 2 tbsp lemon juice
- 2 tbsp olive oil

There are 2 easy ways to roast eggplant (aubergine). One is a little more high maintenance. The first way is to pre-heat an oven to high (400F 200C). You can either place your eggplant in there whole. Or if you have a large eggplant and need to use half of it, cut it down the center, place it cut-side down on a lined baking sheet.

Bake your eggplant for 30-35 minutes. Just check at 25 minutes.

The other way is to place the fruit directly onto a flame on your gas stove or barbecue. As the skin chars, move the fruit to a new uncooked part. You leave the stalk on the aubergine and use it to rotate.

Remove the eggplant from the oven (or stove) and scoop out the flesh. It should be very soft and fall apart when you handle it. You won't be using the skin.

Mix all the ingredients together. I prefer to mash my eggplant and mix everything together rather than have my 'baba' too smooth. It will depend on how soft your roasted eggplant is and your personal preference. So use a fork or pulse or blend with a food processor (or blender).

~ • ~

123. Red Hot Chilli Dip

Do you like hot spicy dips? Then this one is delicious. If you don't like hot peppers (chillis) then leave it out or substitute another spice.

My daughter doesn't like the spicy variety but spreads the plain version on to cucumber slices and makes little cucumber sandwiches.

- 1 cup raw cashews soaked and drained
- 1/2 cup sun dried tomatoes (reserve the water just in case) (or better still, use "Homemade Semi-Dried Tomatoes"
- 1 red capsicum (red bell pepper) seeded
- 1/2 red chilli (deseeded and chopped) leave it out if you want a mild dip
- 1/4 cup olive oil
- Sea salt and pepper to taste

Blend all ingredients until smooth adding the oil little by little to get the desired consistency. Add as much chilli as you like (with or without the seeds).

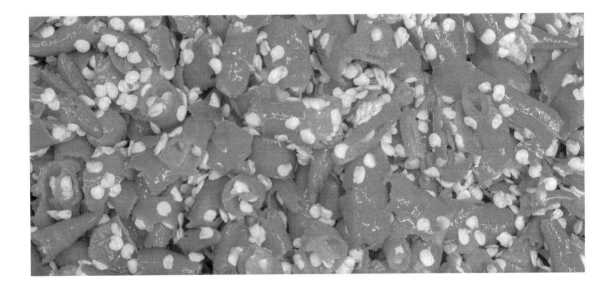

~ • ~

124. Dollop Sweet Cream
(and 7 sweet and savory variations)

Don't be fooled. This non-dairy cream is so versatile. You may think it belongs only as a dessert or covering fruit salad. But I encourage you to try it on other salads. I created Variation 4 (with black pepper and cinnamon and cumin) and was so delighted with the result. It is delectable.

Dates give this cream a lovely uncomplicated sweet taste. While I do like dates, if you prefer to use something with a better nutritional profile then go with soaked dried peaches or apricots. Yes it will change the flavor but then you'll have a different taste sensation too.

The great thing: All of the variations below are excellent desserts, dips for fruit and dressings for savory AND sweet salads. Robert and I love it on the "Fenn-tacular Salad". Be adventurous!

The sea salt is essential to balance the sweetness. The spices in the variations create depth to the flavor.

This is great with plain crackers, a quick sweet treat all on its own, added to fruit salad, muesli, and as I said, with savory salads.

Basic Dollop Sweet Cream Recipe

- 1 cup raw nuts or seeds, soaked, rinsed, drained (cashews are my first choice, but you can use macadamias, pine nuts, sesame or sunflower seeds)
- 2/3 cup coconut water or plain water
- Sweeten with 4 pitted medjool dates
- 1/4 tsp sea salt

Place all your ingredients in the blender and then process until smooth. The proportion of fluid should make your cream thick. If you want to thin it add more coconut water (or water).

Options and variations

For a thicker dollop consistency start with just 1/2 cup of (coconut) water instead of 2/3.

Instead of dates use:

- a small amount of agave or maple syrup
- or 4 soaked dried apricots or 3 dried peach halves (use the soak water as part of your 2/3 cup).

I really like this family-favorite recipe. I tested so many variations and added them to fruit salads and to savory salads. The result is consistently delicious. Your imagination and creativity will be sure to inspire you to mix and match your flavors. Let me know your favorites.

124a. Variation 1 - Coconut Dollop Cream

- Make up some to all of your water component with coconut cream

124b. Variation 2 - Gingered Dollop Cream

- Add 1 tsp of freshly grated ginger

124c. Variation 3 - Sweetly Spiced Dollop Cream

- 1/2 tsp cinnamon
- 1/2 tsp nutmeg
- 1/2 tsp ginger powder
- With or without vanilla

124d. Variation 4 - Peppered Spicy Dollop Cream

- 1/4 tsp or more of freshly ground black pepper
- 1/4 tsp cinnamon
- 1/4 tsp cumin

124e. Variation 5 - Spiced Apricot Dollop Cream

- If you have some "Spiced Apricot Vinaigrette" prepared, take 1-2 tablespoon and mix it in with Dollop Sweet Cream to make a sweet, sour and spicy creamy dressing.

124f. Variation 6 – Vanilla Dollop Cream

- Add a teaspoon of vanilla (with or without ginger)

124g. Variation 7 – Black Pepper Vanilla

- Add vanilla and black pepper generously (with or without ginger)

~ • ~

Garnishes And Snacks

~ • ~

~ • ~

125. Pâtés for Nori or Sushi Rolls or Any Kind of Wrap

Sushi or nori rolls are a perfect vehicle and a superb way to use any or all of your dip selection. Naturally you'll want to keep them a little thicker by paying attention to the amount of fluid you add. You may want to blend your pâtés less to keep them more coarse ... sort of rice consistency.

Layer in your other vegetables, tofu, tempeh or your other favorite fillers, roll it up and really enjoy the difference - in taste, nutrition and the way you feel afterward. You may never go back to rice-filled nori.

Use any of the hummus and especially the pâté recipes to spread on nori (toasted or raw) seaweed sheets. Use it instead of (not as well as) cooked rice.

Prepare your vegetables. I prefer a selection of strips, grated and diced components.

Use one or 2 different complementary dip or pâté creations.

Assembling nori rolls or wraps of any kind

- Choose sauces, dressings or dips that are fairly thick
- Spread on a piece of nori, a lettuce leaf or a flat bread
- Add your vegetables, herbs and leaves of choice
- Add a protein source such as tofu, tempeh (marinated?)
- Add pickles, hot peppers, wasabi if desired
- Wrap or roll up and enjoy your creation

Get inspired by these ingredients and add anything else you like:

- Grate or julienned cut a range of vegetables
- Carrot
- Zucchini
- Snowpeas
- Red pepper (capsicum)
- Radishes
- Lettuce and other leafy greens
- Avocado
- Use strips of tofu or tempeh or if you desire, fish or meat strips
- Pop in some sprouts

126a. Mineral Sprinkles

Buy any assortment of seaweeds. For example: Dulse, Alaria, Kelp, Nori, Wakame, Arame, Laver.

- Grind them together until you achieve a fairly fine powdery texture
- Try using a Vitamix or Blendtec Blender – see my Kitchen Resources Recommendations (with handy links!) here:
- http://www.hotyogadoctor.com/kitchen-resources
- Sprinkle this on anything you like!

Store in a glass jar. It's a great complement to any dinner table and adds the most amazing minerals to your meal. If you're not using iodized sea salt (which is not great nutritionally because it lacks essential minerals and electrolytes for optimal body function) then you want to make sure you are getting your iodine from natural sources.

Sea vegetables are an excellent source (with an excellent amino acid and fatty acid profile too). Plus sea vegetables are at the bottom of the food chain so there is evidence to suggest that the likelihood of contamination is lower. Good news!

126b. Mineral Sesame Sprinkles

A highly nutritious garnish! The Japanese call their version of this Gomasio (pronounced Gomma-sheeo)

- To an assortment of medium coarsely ground seaweeds add
- Sea salt
- Blend your seaweeds first to powder (not too fine)
- Then add your sea salt and process by PULSING the machine
- Now liberally add sesame seeds (black or white seeds or a mixture)

Vary your recipe to taste

Add to anything! Garnish dips and salads.

~ • ~

127. Tomato Chips & Tomato Powder

Whenever my local organic store has tomatoes on for a special price I buy a lot and then make these simply wonderful "Tomato Chips", some "Tomato Powder" and some "Homemade Semi-Dried Tomatoes".

I have tried to avoid use of a dehydrator for this book because it is definitely something that you are unlikely to find in every kitchen. So instead I will give you directions for using both a regular kitchen oven and a dehydrator!

If you have a dehydrator (and even if you don't!)

People like to use dehydrators for many reasons. Raw foodists love them because you can keep the temperature down to a level considered to preserve many of the components that get destroyed by high heat cooking. That level is variously reported around 110-115F and low 43-46 C.

For regular oven use

For regular oven use, just put your oven on the lowest setting.

If you are inclined to keep the temperature down to 'raw foodist' levels, then you will leave the door slightly ajar. If you're not concerned, just leave the door closed and leave the oven on low!

You won't have the fine temperature control of a dehydrator but you will produce delicious morsels that could even seduce you to buy a dehydrator. So look at it as a stepping stone. Even without being a raw foodie a dehydrator is great because it is a cost-saving device. Regular ovens can be expensive to use for very long periods of time.

Here's the recipe

- Slice a couple of pounds of tomatoes into 1/8 inch slices (3 mm).
- Place all the slices on the Teflex sheets close but not overlapping.
- The ends of the tomatoes should be placed skin side down (like little boats).
- Sprinkle with a little sea salt
- Place in the dehydrator for 10-14 hours at about 110F
- Take them out when little dry disks which easily peel off the sheet.

What to do with your chips

Reserve some as snacks that taste like little crisp-ish tomato chips. These are a favorite with all children. Our daughter takes them to school.

Grind the rest up into a fine powder.

Options and variations

- Sea salt is added to the fruit on the tray.
- If you want to add fresh herbs, shred or mince them and sprinkle them over the tray.
- Dry herbs could be added after the dehydration process.
- If you do want to add more than just a sprinkle of salt (and herbs) then it may be easier and less messy to gently combine the ingredients, including the tomatoes, together in a bowl to incorporate and coat the flavors, before laying the tomatoes on the tray.
- Here's what you can add: Herbs, cayenne, paprika, a little agave or even a sprinkle of coconut palm or rapadura sugar.

Hint

If you leave them in long enough you will NOT have to turn them over. They're easy to simply peel off. What I usually do is pop them in the dehydrator in the early evening. Then I check them the next morning.

If they are not sufficiently dry I will then peel them off the sheets and place them on the tray (no sheet) and finish the drying process, which only takes another hour or so (maximum).

Once powdered, you will use these to sprinkle on your pasta dishes or salads. It is SIMPLY FANTASTICALLY DELICIOUS!

~ • ~

128. Homemade Semi-Dried Tomatoes

Semi-dried tomatoes are incredibly versatile. Yes they are wonderful as a salad ingredient. Although they don't appear to be a dressing or a dip (!) they definitely pack a powerful and delectable flavor punch to add to many of your creations including pâtés, dips, salads and wraps.

Garnish with them, dress up your salad with tomato wedges, soak them and blend them up with the soak water to beautifully enhance dressings and dips. If you store them in oil, then that oil will take on a marvelously rich and full flavor.

You will either need an oven on the lowest of settings or to use a dehydrator. If you're a raw foodie then you aim to keep the temperature to about 115F maximum. If you want to do this with your kitchen oven then you drop the temp as far as you can and you can choose to keep the oven door slightly ajar.

Not concerned about the temperature? Then keep the oven door closed.

The taste will be awesome as long as the cooking is slow and at low temperatures. This process concentrates the heavenly flavors. If you get hooked on dehydrating then so be it.

- Start by cutting your fruit into wedges (not slices).
- You can also choose cherry or baby Roma tomatoes and cut them in half.

Simply Salted

- Sprinkle the tomato wedges with sea salt and place them on the sheets (skin down) like little boats

Marinated

Prepare a quick marinade:

- Olive oil
- Sea salt
- Pepper
- Garlic
- Just a little dash of Bragg Liquid Aminos/apple cider vinegar/lemon juice/balsamic vinegar
- Add a little unprocessed rapadura or coconut palm sugar which creates a great rounded flavor to balance the acid nature of the toms
- Test the taste of your mix

Gently toss the tomato wedges in the marinade and then lay them out onto the dehydrator sheets, skin-side down.

Dehydrate 2 hours, then check

The time in the dehydrator depends on the size of the wedges and the desired dryness of the resulting product. Start with 2 hours at 110 Fahrenheit and then extend the time as required.

Remove from oven

Take your wedges out of the dehydrator.

Storing

If you're planning on using them that meal then you are done. However if you have a large output of tomatoes then you may need to store them under olive oil.

While you would use a fair amount of your chosen oil, the great news is that you have tomato flavored oil to create beautiful salad dressings and vinaigrettes. Use this oil for any dressing you desire.

Hint for storing

Place a layer of tomatoes and a little oil. Continue to layer and add oil. This will avoid creating pockets of air. And ultimately use less oil than piling all the pieces into a jar first.

129. Simple Tomato Snack

Just a simple idea to use any of your pâtés or dips to make a great snack that is and isn't a salad! Maybe you will use a selection of sliced veggies: Cucumbers, fine slices of carrot, some bell pepper. Your imagination is your limitation.

- Choose any pâté
- Tomato in 1/8 - 1/4 inch slices
- Spread with pesto on top (pine nut, basil, garlic, olive oil and salt)
- Top with alfalfa or other sprout and some sliced kalamata olives

130. Open Cucumber Sandwiches

- 1/2 large cucumber, cut into 1/8 -1/4 inch slices
- Spread with any paté
- Top with an herb sprig or olive

Kids love these as a 'closed' cucumber sandwich

Toppings for your salads

Anything goes!

Nuts, seeds, herbs and spices are all wonderful ways to garnish your dressed salad or decorate your dip, pâté, hummus, pesto, salsa, cream or guacamole.

You can decoratively cut some vegetable. Add some wedges of lime or lemon to squeeze on at the plate. How about a curl of celery, some flower shaped carrot slices or some julienned cucumber? Even diced veggies will do the trick.

Sprinkle with caraway seeds, different color ground peppercorns.

You will either choose an item that you're already using in that recipe, or go for color, texture or taste impact to complement or even juxtapose what's there. If for example you have a totally green salad, think about garnishing with a splash of red.

Here is a list of specific ideas to enhance your dishes:

131. Superbly Spiced Sprinkles

To combine nuts or seeds with a little spice, salt and sweetness is a tasty garnish. How you do it depends on you. You can add these sprinkles without any cooking or preparation beyond mixing the ingredients together.

You can dry the mix out a little in a dehydrator or oven too. Dry frying nuts and seeds to heat and lightly toast them accentuates the nuttiness. It will also set the syrup a little.

- 1/4 cup hazelnuts, chopped
- 1/4 tsp cumin powder (or coriander powder)
- 2 tsp agave, maple syrup or honey
- A pinch of sea salt

Options and variations

Substitutions:

- Change the cumin for cinnamon
- Change the nuts for sunflower seeds

How about trying:

Chopped macadamias and almonds

Almonds, maple, salt and cinnamon

Cranberries, sunflower seeds, salt and honey

Tamari, sunflower seeds

Almonds, sunflower seeds, tamari and cranberries

In any of these garnishes use the suggested variations above.

Coconut shreds, coconut flakes

Raw or toasted (dry fried or crisped in the oven).

~ • ~

132. Surprise Me Cheesy Sprinkles

So what's the big surprise? Well, it's cheesy ... but there's no cheese. You could call this Faux Cheese. Or maybe Parmesan Cheezy Powder. I once tasted this at a café and was amazed. To me the taste of the yeast flakes is quite addictive. So adding macadamia nuts for me makes this a winner - nutritionally and deliciously! To me it's irresistible.

- 1/4 tsp sea salt
- 1/4 cup macadamias
- 2 tbsp yeast flakes (or nutritional yeast works too). Metric tablespooners use 1.5.

Use a grinder, hand grater or blender to create a ground/powdered nut dust. Not too fine. It's good to have a little texture.

- Pulse with the sea salt if the salt needs to be ground at all.
- Add the yeast.
- Taste test. Adjust the salt and yeast to taste.
- Serve over any salad. Use as a garnish. Heck, I just eat this by the spoonful.

You may need to just double up or triple up the amounts!

Chia Seeds

Want to add something highly nutritious that goes with any taste, sweet, sour, bitter or salty, without changing the profile of your chosen recipe?

Add chia seeds.

Chia seeds have loads of protein, calcium, fiber and omega-3s (and more!). Because of their neutral flavor you can add them as a sprinkling garnish. But there are better ways to get the nutrition.

When chia seeds are mixed in water they plump up. In fact they absorb about 7 times their weight (and some say more) of water. When you place 1 tablespoon of chia in a jar and add about 5-6 tablespoons of water, stir and wait 20 minutes, you will end up with a 'chia gel'. It keeps for a week in the fridge.

Here's something you may not know about chia gel. While you will benefit from the dietary fiber, some protein and the interesting mouth-feel (that is rather like tapioca pearls) there is scientific evidence that shows that in order to unlock the protein (etc) you need to break them down.

So if you're adding chia for its nutrition then either pulverize to a powder or add chia gel and then blend.

Yes you will get nutrition out of the whole seed whether dry or gel but its potential will only be unlocked in the ground state, especially if it's raw. The components become more 'bioavailable'. That bioavailability changes from under 25% to over 90%.

The texture of chia gel is very pleasant. It's very useful to give body to a dressing. If you make a vinaigrette and it's too thin, add a tablespoon or so of gel.

Taste your dressing. If it becomes too thick you can thin it down with a touch of water or more oil.

So, if you're spending the money on chia seeds primarily for their nutrition then consider blending them. For the best of both worlds: You can blend some and add some 'chia gel' for the mouth-feel.

The Lists Of Salad Ingredients

These lists could go on and on for pages. That's partly why I put them at the end of the book! What you really want to 'get' from this is that there are so many things that you can have in your salads that the possibilities, the combinations, the meals are literally endless. I don't know about you, but for me that is really inspiring.

You could be someone who likes to stick to favorites and you can eat them time and time again. I can pretty much guarantee that, unless you have an eating obsession of some kind, that your favorites do change. Your eating habits do evolve.

Just cast your eye down the list and even extract from it the ones that you love and like. Maybe you'll 'rediscover' some ingredients that you like that you haven't used in ages. I do know that when you pair your salads - any salad - with delicious dressings that you'll end up eating things that could even be far down on your list.

That in itself could complete your nutrition needs by including different veggies you haven't paid much attention to over the years!

Groups of salad ingredients include:

- Herbs
- Seeds
- Nuts

- Sea vegetables (seaweeds great to sprinkle as a powder: see "Garnishes And Snacks")
- Oils and Vinegars
- Vegetables
- Tofu and tempeh
  (Flesh products and dairy and eggs as you desire them. Please see notes here: "Tofu and tempeh")

The following lists are just a small portion of the choices available to you.

Tree fruit

- Apple
- Apricot
- Cherries
- Figs
- Kiwi
- Nectarine
- Peach
- Pear
- Plum

Citrus fruit

- Lemon
- Lime
- Orange
- Tangerine
- Mandarin
- Grapefruit

Tropical and exotic

- Avocado
- Dates
- Durian
- Guava
- Jackfruit
- Kiwi
- Lychee
- Mango
- Nashi pear
- Mangosteen
- Passionfruit
- Pawpaw or Papaya

- Persimmon
- Pineapple
- Rambutan
- Salak
- Tamarind

Vegetables – Common Varieties Including Fruit That Are Considered As Vegetables

Fruit Vegetables

- Avocados
- Cucumbers
- Courgette or zucchini (summer squash)
- Eggplant
- Okra
- Olives
- Peppers
- Squash (and pumpkin varieties)
- Tomatoes
- Tomatillos

Herbs are part of the vegetable family. Here's a short list

- Basil
- Chives
- Cilantro
- Dill
- Garlic chives
- Lemon balm
- Oregano
- Parsley
- Rosemary
- Sage
- Sorrel
- Tarragon
- Thyme

Leafy and other types of vegetables

- Artichokes
- Arugula or rocket
- Asparagus

- Beans
- Broccoli
- Brussels sprouts
- Cabbage
- Cauliflower
- Celery
- Chard
- Chicory
- Chinese cabbage
- Collards
- Dandelion nettles
- Endive
- Fennel
- Lamb's lettuce
- Kale (many varieties)
- Kohlrabi
- Lettuce (many varieties)
- Mizuna
- Nasturtium
- Purslane
- Rocket
- Radicchio
- Savoy
- Sea kale
- Sorrel
- Spinach
- Sprouts of all kinds, seeds, nuts, beans, vegetables etc
- Watercress

Bulb, Root and Tuber Vegetables

- Beets
- Burdock
- Carrots
- Celeriac
- Chives
- Garlic
- Jerusalem artichoke
- Jicama
- Leeks
- Onions
- Parsnips
- Potato
- Radishes

- Scallions
- Shallots
- Sweet potato
- Rutabaga
- Salsify
- Taro
- Turnips
- Water chestnuts
- Yam

Nuts and Seeds

- Almonds
- Brazil
- Cacao (woo hoo! Unprocessed natural chocolate)
- Cashew
- Chestnuts
- Coconut
- Flax
- Hazelnut or Filberts
- Macadamias
- Peanuts
- Pecans
- Pine nuts
- Pistachios
- Pumpkin seeds
- Sesame seeds
- Sunflower seeds
- Walnuts

Miscellaneous

- Hmmm ... mushrooms don't fit into any of the other categories. And neither do all the sea vegetables! Here they are. There are many varieties of each.
- Miso

Oils and Vinegars and Condiments

Just about every nut and seed can be used as an oil in the kitchen. Some are more commonly used than others. Some like sesame seeds are used ground up creating a paste of the flesh and oil into a product variously called tahina or tahini. Both names can and are used in, and you'll find both in this book.

As in all your food choices if you can, you would be best to buy organic products. But probably the most important is to buy goods that are processed minimally if at all, and with best practice. For oils and nut and see butters that means COLD PRESSED, with no heating used at all.

The nutrition value of cold pressed oils is far greater than oils prepared with heat or via other methods. Some manufacturers will use heat to hull or dehusk or open nuts and seeds. This can render the enzymes and vitamin content inactive and can also contribute to product degradation.

Heat is often used because it makes the process faster and cheaper for big business, so that's why cold pressed or thoughtfully processed food is more expensive.

There are some oils that you will use in small amounts. They are great to have in your cupboard because of their nutritional value.

Here are the oils that I use

I am listing them in alphabetical order:

Apricot Kernel Oil

- I use this from time to time sparingly, because it's good to use different oils. This one is very mild tasting and has a good profile with a mix of beneficial elements (including mono- and polyunsaturated fats (omega 6 and 9) It also contains vitamin B17 which is reputed to have postulated anti-cancer qualities. It is present in quite a number of raw foods but is particularly high in apricot kernels. If you believe it has magic properties, then use it. Equally, if you believe it's good to use a variety of quality oils (even without the marketing hype) then use it! Never use just one oil. This one won't be your main oil.

Avocado Oil

- A rich green oil that you can decoratively drizzle on dips and salads (or in them). It is high in monounsaturated fatty acids and a good source of vitamin E and potassium.

Coconut oil

- A very distinctive flavor and because of its high burning temperature it's one of the few oils you can cook with. Touted as one of the best oils to use raw, in food and on the skin. I use it as face and body 'cream'. Coconut is considered an excellent superfood.

Extra Virgin Olive Oil

- A kitchen essential that is proven healthy and tastes great. There are many varieties with different flavors due to the differently timed harvests of different fruit. 'EVOO' is very versatile because it is delicious raw and can also be cooked with. It is best to confine this oil to lower heat when cooking with it. A fantastic all-rounder.

Flaxseed Oil

- Flaxseed oil really ought to be part of your kitchen supplies. I keep it in the fridge to preserve nutrition and stay fresh. It should come to you in a dark or opaque bottle. It has a high level of omega 3 fatty acids, is indicated for people with inflammatory conditions. It has a unique flavor that can be nutty and mild. If it is too strong or fishy then it is possibly rancid. If you buy a big amount then store the unused portion in the freezer. Just use this stuff raw. Don't cook with it. Pour it over things, even 'butter' your toast with it, but frying with it is a big no-no.

Hazelnut Oil

- A mild tasting nutty oil with sweet notes very high in monounsaturated fats.

Macadamia Oil

- Mild tasting, a different profile, great for salads and occasional frying. I don't fry with this. When I buy pricey oils I use them raw for maximum nutritional value.

Pumpkin seed oil

- Great in salads, dark color, rich flavor. Highly nutritious with a good balance of essential fatty acids and rich in iron, magnesium, potassium and zinc. Very nice to splash a decorative swirl onto hummus.

Sesame Oil (including Black Sesame Oil)

- Most commercially available sesame oils are from toasted seeds. For best nutrition you would buy raw, cold pressed. If you like the toasted sesame oil taste buy toasted oil and add it sparingly maybe using the raw one as the major component. I do that! I like to use black sesame oil raw for its calcium, iron, copper, magnesium, phosphorus and zinc, and its essential fatty acid profile.

Sunflower Oil

- I use this one for salads but also particularly because it is one of the cheapest organic cold pressed oils that is suitable for cooking (frying) which we do sometimes! If I do fry something in oil then I don't want to be throwing away expensive oils and literally burning up some of their great nutritive value.

Udo's Oil

- This oil is a blend of different plant-based oils from organic sources that is said to provide the perfect blend of essential fatty acids. You only ever use this one raw, never heat it. It has a pleasant flavor.

Walnut Oil

- A wonderful source of omega-3 fatty acids and many minerals and vitamins (especially the B group). It has a nutty flavor which I really enjoy in salad dressings. It's really best suited to keeping it raw.

Vinegars and Amino Sauces

The following sauces can be used interchangeably with any vinegars for many of the recipes in this book. You will establish your favorites no doubt. Keep the intention of the recipe you are making in mind. Know the flavor of your vinegars and sauces so that you can be easily inspired to experiment.

Apple cider vinegar

- I use Bragg organic and unfiltered apple cider vinegar. There are other varieties. I just buy the big bottle and keep decanting it into a smaller one in the kitchen.

Balsamic vinegar

- Many different qualities available. They tend to be sweeter. Varieties can be thin and watery right through to thick and syrupy.

Bragg Liquid Aminos

- My favorite soy sauce because it tastes good and doesn't overpower the food you add it to. I have discovered too via experimentation, that it can be used as a substitute for fish sauce so it's great in Thai food.

Coconut aminos

- Made from coconut with another excellent amino acid profile. It has a sweetish salty taste with a slight spicy feel. Try using it as a substitute for Bragg Liquid Aminos. Or substitute it for vinegar too.

Hot red pepper sauce

- No you can't buy it but it's one of my favorite things: Just chop up hot chilli peppers small and marinate them in Bragg Liquid Aminos, coconut aminos or tamari. I chop enough to half fill a jar and keep topping up the Bragg to freshen it up the sauce. Lasts for weeks. The Bragg or tamari becomes spicy and you can choose to use the liquid, the chilli or both.

Soy sauce

- This to me is the most overpowering of soy sauces. It tends to dominate a recipe especially if it's overused. I never use it anymore because of this characteristic. I much prefer Bragg.

Tamari

- Wheat free soy sauce. I consider this to be a halfway house between soy and Bragg. Very lovely in Asian dressings and making toppings with seeds and nuts to garnish your salads and dips.

Vinegars

- Try making any of the dressing recipes taste completely different by using different vinegars than those listed.

Wine vinegars

- You can find red and white wine vinegars everywhere. They are very popular. The better the quality of the wine vinegar the better the dressing will taste.

Thank you!

I truly hope you have enjoyed discovering or rediscovering the joy of salads, dressings, dips. Oh, and salsas, guacamoles, garnishes and creams.

Here is my promise to you

If there's any stone unturned I will turn it for you. Any typos, I will fix them. Any ideas to improve, I will implement them! ... either in this or in my future or other recipe books.

It's important to me to make high quality products. Seems incredible but because of technology I have the opportunity to instantly fix the e-book and even the print book within a few days. So this means, if you find something I have overlooked then I want to hear about it.

So remember, send me feedback, suggestions and things to fix. I promise to take every word seriously.

Your email will come directly to ME, not some go-between or gatekeeper. Here's my email address: info@hotyogadoctor.com.

Disclaimer

This is a book with many recipes. I love creating great meals for my family and friends. I wrote this book so I could share my hints, tips, recipes and creations so that you too can incorporate more fruit, vegetables, nuts, seeds and leafy green vegetables into your life. Who knows what kind of magic will happen in your life as a result of mindful nutrition?

This book makes no warranties, guarantees or promises to heal any illness nor does it promise that it will keep you young, make you look better, feel better, cure diseases, prevent diseases or stop the symptoms or signs of conditions or illnesses.

If you have questions about your own state of health it is always a good idea to consult people whom you trust, medicos, other health professionals or even a nutritional consultant. Perhaps you need to be reminded to 'consult your physician'.

Enjoy your discovery into introducing (more) salads into your eating plans. Make it your way of life and it's extremely likely that you will be rewarded!

And... if you've enjoyed even just some of the salads and dressings and dips in this book, then I would greatly appreciate a positive review!

A friendly request!

Positive reviews from people like you are important for me and my ability to keep on creating!

If you have enjoyed and maybe even loved this book (I hope so) then please leave a 4 or 5 (!) star review.

If for some reason you think this book deserves less than 4 stars, and I need to do more to earn a great review from you then I make what could appear to be a cheeky request. And that is, instead of leaving that review I request that you please contact me with your feedback directly so I can make amends! You can reach me personally at info@hotyogadoctor.com. I take all feedback seriously!

This is me with my salad-loving daughter ;)

Thank you in advance for your review!

And here's a handy link to the review page:

http://www.amazon.com/dp/B00BQTE3PW

4931202R00117